THINGS YOU NEED TO HEAR

Things You Need to Hear

Collected Memories of Growing Up in Arkansas, 1890–1980

MARGARET JONES BOLSTERLI

The University of Arkansas Press
Fayetteville
2012

ISBN-10: 1-55728-978-6
ISBN-13: 978-1-55728-978-0

16 15 14 13 12   5 4 3 2 1

Designed by Liz Lester

♾ The paper used in this publication meets the minimum requirements of the American National Standard for Permanence of Paper for Printed Library Materials Z39.48-1984.

LIBRARY OF CONGRESS CATALOGING-IN-PUBLICATION DATA

Bolsterli, Margaret Jones.
    Things you need to hear : collected memories of growing up in Arkansas, 1890/1980 / Margaret Jones Bolsterli.
        p.   cm.
    Includes index.
    ISBN-13: 978-1-55728-978-0 (cloth : alk. paper)
    ISBN-10: 1-55728-978-6 (cloth : alk. paper)
        1. Arkansas—History—Anecdotes. 2. Arkansas—Biography—Anecdotes. 3. Arkansas—Social life and customs—Anecdotes. 4. Interviews—Arkansas. 5. Oral history—Arkansas. I. Title.
        F411.6.B65   2012
        976.7—dc23

                                                                2011044831

Publication of this book was supported by the Old State House Museum in Little Rock, Arkansas, whose exhibit of the same name was curated by the author.

Excerpts from *Womenfolks* by Shirley Abbott, 1983, Ticknor & Fields; copyright © 1983 by Shirley Abbott; reprinted by permission of Shirley Abbott. Excerpts from *I Know Why the Caged Bird Sings* by Maya Angelou; copyright © 1969 and renewed 1997 by Maya Angelou; used by permission of Random House, Inc. Excerpts from *The Boy From Altheimer: From the Depression to the Boardroom* by William H. Bowen; copyright © 2006 by the University of Arkansas Press; reprinted by permission of the University of Arkansas Press. Excerpts from pp. 12–21, 52–53 from *Cash: The Autobiography* by Johnny Cash and Patrick Carr; copyright © 1997 by John R. Cash; reprinted by permission of HarperCollins Publishers. Excerpts from pp. 13–24, 42 from *This Wheel's on Fire* by Levon Helm and Stephen Davis; copyright © 1993 by Levon Helm and Stephen Davis; reprinted by permission of HarperCollins Publishers. Excerpts from *Cotton Field of Dreams: A Memoir* by Janis F. Kearney, Writing Our World Press; copyright © 2004 by Janis F. Kearney; reprinted by permission of Janis F. Kearney. Excerpts from *William Grant Still and the Fusion of Cultures in American Music*, Black Sparrow Press, Los Angeles 1972; copyright © William Grant Still, all rights reserved (williamgrantstill.com); reprinted by permission of Judith Anne Still, William Grant Still Music. Excerpts from "Interview with Billy Lee Riley," by Jeannie Whayne; *The Arkansas Historical Quarterly*, vol. LV, no. 3, Autumn, 1996.

For Betsy, Raymond, Emily, Joy, Fritz, Biddley, Jody,
Teddy, George, Dan, and Margaret, who live in
my own memories of growing up in Arkansas

CONTENTS

FOREWORD

In 2005 an exhibit devoted to growing up in Arkansas was added to the Old State House Museum exhibit schedule. The next step was to find a curator. The museum was fortunate in securing the skills of Dr. Margaret Bolsterli, a native Arkansan widely known for her expertise as an interpreter of the history of the state and region. Her task began with the selection of the interviewees and ended in the publication of this book and installation of an exhibit at the Old State House.

Bolsterli relates the experience of growing up in Arkansas through the reminiscences of forty-one individuals. Included here are memories of selected Arkansans who grew up in different parts of the state. Collectively these memories reveal much about the culture and society of the state—and changes that occurred in both over time.

The oral histories collected here are amazingly comprehensive in exploring a variety of themes abundantly evident in the Arkansas experience. Such themes include class, race, education, family values, religion, child rearing, economic development, and cultural life. Bolsterli's sources are male and female, black and white, advantaged and disadvantaged, and they share their childhoods growing up in Arkansas during the period between 1890 and 1980. She gives special attention to communication between family members and how electronic media have changed that internal family dialog.

Issues featured in this work are familiar to many of us. Margaret Bolsterli has placed them in an Arkansas context that makes them especially fascinating to Arkansans and students of the rural South.

BILL GATEWOOD

ACKNOWLEDGMENTS

I was delighted to accept Bill Gatewood's invitation to write a book and curate an exhibit at the Old State House Museum on growing up in Arkansas because I happened to have a drawer full of taped interviews on that very subject that I had made over the years for other projects. Since the thought of wasting material is anathema to me, I leapt at the chance to use some of those records. My oldest informants, taped in 1986, were born in the 1890s, and one of them, Lily Peter, could remember events from 1894. My next round of interviews was made in 1997 with informants born in the first half of the twentieth century. In order to bring this study into the 1970s, in 2009 I began a new set of recordings with people born between 1950 and 1960. I enjoyed every single conversation and am deeply grateful for the willingness of these informants to talk about incidents in their childhood and adolescence that were sometimes still painful to recall. In addition, I am grateful for the written statements I received from several people whom I could not reach with a tape recorder.

To supplement my own work, I added excerpts from three visual interviews made by Scott Lunsford for the David and Barbara Pryor Center for Arkansas Oral and Visual History. They add immeasurably to the whole project. Kris Katrosh, director of the Pryor Center, was most helpful in getting those materials to me.

In addition, I used excerpts from the published memoirs of several well-known Arkansans.

I regret that there is no way for the printed word to show the rich variety of tone and accent of speech from different parts of the state that add to the pleasures of conversing with Arkansans, but trying to replicate the sounds on the page would have meant sinking in the quicksand of written dialect.

Marie Demeroukas at the Shiloh Museum of Ozark History was invaluable in finding useful photographs for me from their massive collection. At Special Collections, University of Arkansas Libraries, Tom Dillard read the manuscript and provided encouragement and good advice when I needed it most. Geoffrey Stark and William Quinn Jr. were helpful in finding and reproducing suitable photographs.

Finally, as they have done for most of my work over the last thirty years or so, Olivia Sordo and the late Willard Gatewood read and reread the evolving manuscripts and offered suggestions so useful I cannot imagine the result without them. I am deeply grateful, as always.

We Remember

An enduring memory from my early childhood is the sound of my mother's soft voice telling about her childhood as she did housework. When it was rainy, or too hot to be outside, or we were sick or bored, my brother and I would nag at her to "tell us what it was like when you were little," and while her hands were busy, she told us stories about her sisters and brothers, parents, grandmothers, cousins, school, poverty, and the joys and struggles of a large family making a living on a hard-acre farm in Ashley County, where they had moved after losing everything they owned in Mississippi during the Civil War. Mother's grandmother from Mississippi had lived with her family and told the children stories about her own childhood that Mother passed on to us. So right there, we had links to three previous generations and the family's history for over a century. And when she ran out of things to tell about her own childhood, she would repeat the stories she had heard about my father's. As an example of the kind of thing that came to mind when she looked up from her work and stared out the window, since we were living on the spot where my father had grown up, she might remark that the trees shading the house grew from walnuts he had dumped from his little wagon as a small boy. And she could tell exactly where at my father's grandfather's house just down the road he had picked up the nuts. It was the same with my father, who also loved to tell stories. His own father had fought in the Civil War, and the family had been in Desha County so long that he knew practically everybody in it and had things to relate about most of them, as well as members of his family who still lived in Tennessee, many of whom he had never even met.

Our imaginations were nourished by these tales about people long gone who seemed as real to us as the members of the family who sat at the table three times a day. It was as if we were always in the presence of three or four generations of our family on each side. There is no question that knowing about them helped shape our definition of who we were.

In the characterizations of the actors in the little dramas related to us there were humor and wisdom and lessons for life. The lazy ones did not get off unscathed and the courageous were honored. If it was at all possible, the teller worked a moral into the story, and if not it was fine to tell one that was simply funny or interesting. Because, while this age-old oral tradition served to pass the culture along to each succeeding generation, the real intention was entertainment, and in our house and many others, it was frequently the only entertainment there was. The first incursion into this way of life, of course, was the arrival of the radio to which people began listening in the evenings in the early 1930s, to the detriment of storytelling. Most people had no electricity until the 1940s, so the radios ran on batteries, and if necessary people took the battery out of the car or truck or tractor so the family could listen for a few hours after supper. But there was still time to talk. In our house, Mother did not listen to the radio while doing housework, and while my father sat on the porch smoking after supper, he would tell stories to anybody who would listen. And we, like most other families, sat down together three times a day for our meals with no distractions except eating and talking.

The case was different after television came along in the late 1940s and people got into the habit of having the TV set on all the time. In addition to that, more and more women began leaving the house for work; there were fewer and fewer at home all day with time to talk to children while their hands were busy. Finally, the advent of the Internet may have landed the final blow to the oral tradition. Even the children no longer have time or inclination to listen to their parents tell stories, if they ever do. At the dinner table, the one place left where the collective wisdom might be passed down by word of mouth, most eyes and ears are focused on a television set. Before and after dinner, attention may also be focused on the computer and other electronic devices. And the truth is that many families no longer share even one meal a day.

Another result of the lure of technology as entertainment is that children no longer play outside in the summers and after school. A visitor from outer space who landed in Arkansas on any given day might think there are no children here, while we native earthlings know where they are: indoors watching television or playing computer games or texting their friends, as ignorant of the lives lived shortly before theirs as they are of the lives of the aliens they love to watch on the screen.

And there are things to be told; there are memories about growing up in Arkansas that are worth repeating both for their intrinsic value and the pleasure in hearing them. For that reason, I have assembled this collective memory of growing up in Arkansas between 1890 and 1980 told by the people who did it. It will tell, in their own words and voices and photographs, what people under the age of eighteen did to get an education, amuse themselves, and earn money before there were television sets and computers to entertain them and fast-food restaurants to employ them.

It must always be remembered that these memories lie within the context of families that existed in communities, and because of the pervasive nature of racism in the social structure of Arkansas, we are describing communities in parallel universes of black and white. One way of comprehending how these two cultures existed side by side, frequently in the same spaces, is to imagine each existing inside a discrete, opaque bubble. Sometimes these bubbles collide with terrible consequences and their differences are remarked with corrosive consequences to all. But also, almost miraculously, sometimes the bubbles merge and black and white are able to see past the obstacles and into each other's culture and understand the human condition involved. The result of this merging in the cases of musicians like Billy Lee Riley and Levon Helm formed part of what is, arguably, the most exciting change in American music in the twentieth century: the melding of white and black style into rockabilly, rock-and-roll, and blues.

The injustices of Jim Crow were apparent to all and sometimes inspired black children to succeed beyond all expectations at fulfilling their dreams. In like measure, those injustices encouraged some white children to grow up to fight for racial equality at the risk of alienating their parents and friends.

Class distinctions and poverty also play a part in our collective memory of childhood, but there is an overwhelming affirmation of hope in the memories of the struggles and the lessons learned from them. For example, Billy Lee Riley, recalling the hard work of following a mule pulling a plow in a cotton field ten hours a day at the age of ten, is also reminded of the sweet aroma of the newly turned soil. Johnny Cash, while telling of the backbreaking labor in the cotton fields near Helena also recollects how pretty the fields were when the new bolls flowered and even that the flowers were sweet enough to eat. Helen Pennington fondly recalls riding to Dumas on Saturday afternoon on top of the newly picked bale of cotton, looking forward to the pleasures of town during harvest time when everybody had a little money and got to go to the movies and have a tuna fish sandwich. Joycelyn Elders in retrospect credits the difficulty of getting good medical attention in her childhood with inspiring her to become a doctor. Jerry Mauldin acknowledges that the slurs he received as a child from the wrong side of the tracks gave him the drive to reach the top of his field. Raymond Riggins is mindful of the way his teacher in a one-room school kept telling him "You are better than you are" to inspire him to achieve. Bill Covey remembers with pleasure attending dances on the highway bridges in Desha County as a teenager because his crowd had no other place to dance.

And there are also thoughts in our collection of more privileged, even idyllic lives. Karen Rudolph Shoffner describes the cotillion in Fayetteville in the 1950s. Sally Stockley Johnson and Joy Hudson tell of playing on the sidewalks in Helena and Dumas with all the other children in the neighborhood from early morning until bedtime.

Delta Willis recalls going frog-gigging in Desha County with her father and his friends and worrying about the cottonmouth moccasins that might get into the boat. LaVerne Feaster recounts the pleasures of attending the different churches in Cotton Plant with her friends on Sundays. Cecile Cazort Zorach tells about getting dressed up on Saturday afternoons to go downtown in Little Rock with her sister and mother to shop. And all remember school, most with pleasure, some with forbearance, and many with regret that they didn't have more opportunities for higher education.

So here are accounts of what some of us did when we were young. This is not meant to be a scientific or sociological study or even a cohesive history, but rather a collection of the memories that several generations of people who grew up in Arkansas have carried from childhood. Since I have written about my own childhood at length in other books, I have tried to stay out of the way and let the others tell what it was like when they were young.

The stories collected here are confined to the period in each person's life before the age of eighteen or graduation from high school. Our oldest informant, Lily Peter, was born in Phillips County in 1892, and when I interviewed her in 1986, she could remember actual events from 1894 and family stories from much earlier times. The youngest, Mike Thomas, who grew up in Washington County, graduated from high school in 1980.

I have tried to arrange these accounts according to five major themes: community, family, work, school, and play, but since minds wander and thoughts resist being confined to boxes, some overlap the boundaries of their classification. I decided to begin with those related to community, the immediate larger world that children knew in order to set the stage for the areas of family, work, school, and play. People may remember other things from childhood, but these five themes are common to all.

I ask the reader to imagine being in a group somewhere with these people, say, in a doctor's waiting room, or a family reunion, or the wake before a funeral, or listening to their parents or grandparents talk, the way Arkansans do when there are a few of us around and there's no television set in the room. If you listen carefully, you will hear the voices of ghosts describing communities and families and customs and habits that no longer exist. You may hear those voices telling you things you need to hear. They may be telling you where you came from and, therefore, who you are.

THINGS YOU NEED TO HEAR

CHAPTER 1

Community and Memory

Since memories of community provide the framework for all the others, the pleasures and pains associated with it form some of the oldest memories that many people carry to their graves. The family, the yard, the house, the workplace, and the school all exist in some kind of community that sets the standards by which children identify themselves. It is their community that provides the comfort of belonging or the stigma of alienation.

In the present era of instant global communication it is hard to imagine the isolation of most rural communities in Arkansas only a short time ago. But it is easy to imagine how the bonds of those communities were strengthened by their isolation in the days before good roads, telephones, and radios. With little coming in from the rest of the world, people had to depend on themselves and neighbors for both help and entertainment, and old ideas died hard when there were so few ways for new ones to get in.

This collection of memories of people who grew up in Arkansas between 1890 and 1980 illuminates the changes in the lives of people brought about by the growth of technology. The oldest among our informants, in rural areas, lived in houses without electricity or running water and depended on horses and horse-drawn vehicles for transportation over dirt or, at best, gravel roads.

Work was done by hand, and the hands of children did a great deal of it. Most had chores around the house and yard, and many did brutal work in fields and canning factories and sawmills for very little pay. No wonder they recall so well the few diversions from work and boredom provided by the meager resources of their communities, like the annual picnics that were looked forward to all year long and remembered into old age for the celebrations they were of visiting and sharing food among people unaccustomed to such variety and abundance of either food or company.

Churches were looked to for the moral backbone they were intended to provide and sometimes served up entertainment as well, disguised as enlightenment in debates over doctrinal differences or observations of different rituals and practices.

In the early years, the local school of eight grades, usually in one room, was a source of interest and fierce pride to everyone from first grade through the previous generations who had attended it. Since they provided one of the main sources of entertainment, school plays, recitations, and spelling bees were a matter of interest to everyone in the community. School consolidation, which began to come in with improved roads in the 1920s and 1930s, changed all this. The small rural communities began to disappear as people began going to nearby towns for school, church, shopping, and jobs.

Formally, churches and schools were the centers of community. Informally, a community consisted of individuals who took responsibility for the common good. Children were watched and sometimes corrected by the nearest adult, and a family in trouble could expect to be helped by other families.

Parallel universes of black and white communities existed side by side in many communities, and racism was present, in some degree, in the consciousness of every single individual in Arkansas. It was like a thick, acrid, poisonous smoke that permeated everything and was breathed by everyone. The memories that African Americans carry affirm that while the pain inflicted by racism may vary in degree, it is an ingredient in them all. The memories of white children who secretly questioned the racial situation in the face of their community and parental norms recall the reinforcement for their doubts that they received in the 1960s on radio and television. This is an indication that by the 1960s the isolation of even the most rural communities was being broken by communication with the outside world. This external reinforcement for their doubts about the racial inequality accepted by their society also reinforced their doubts about the wisdom of every single authority figure most of them had ever known. Yet in spite of the presence of virulent racism, the memories of many in both races bear witness to a remarkable number of cases of rapprochement between black and white children.

In addition to the minefield of race, matters of class also had to be negotiated. Town people looked down on country people and the less fortunate. It was apparent to some children that language was a marker of social class, and if learning the grammar and tone of upper-class speech was necessary to move up in the social scale, they were willing to make a conscious effort to do it.

Community was a palpable thing, an overreaching arbiter of taste and behavior that was extremely important to the formation of personality and character. The other clusters of memory, like those involved with family, work, school, and play, existed within it

Leta Drake Parker

b. 1917, Drake's Creek, rural Madison County.
Interview with Margaret Bolsterli, 1997.

I was conceived in the weaner house in my granddad's yard. A weaner house is a little bitty house that kids lived in when they first got married until they [their folks] could wean them off.

We had a close feeling of community. Over there on Cobb Branch, every Easter they had the biggest iron kettle I ever saw, and everybody in the country brought a dozen or two eggs, and poured them in there and we boiled them. And we all had other food that we brought, and we had a dinner and that lasted until after I was grown.

And we'd go to revivals at Draketown. The Church of Christ people and the Baptists used to have arguments about their religious faith. And I'll never forget what one fellow said when they got through with their debating and he went to get a drink and picked up a dipper of water and looked in it and threw it out and said, "Good lands! There's one of those big old Baptist bugs in my water." We had a little church and Sunday school up there most of the time, and the people then used to stay all night with each other, and we ate with them every time they came by.

We made our entertainment, and for entertainment aside from the meetings and like that, we would have "tacky parties" and then we had "apron parties," and that was where the girl took an apron that wasn't hemmed and the boy hemmed it. The boy drew the girl's name, and whoever he got, he had to hem that apron. We just had a lot of fun, had to walk wherever we went, mostly, but later on my dad bought a hack. We didn't get out much because my mother wasn't well, but one time we went to the circus. That's the first time I ever heard of a circus being in Madison County, and they had it at Draketown.

I miss that kind of community; I think it's gone forever. When I was a child, there were no TVs. There were no radios, and all the entertainment we had was just what we did with each other. At the Draketown Hotel, Oliver Neal and Minnie, his wife, got the first radio that was ever in the country, and I think I was thirteen when that happened. And back then you didn't ask anybody if you could come to their house. If you wanted to go, you just went. So on Saturday night all of us teenagers would gang up in their front room, and we just barely had room for everybody that came. They had a big fireplace, and they built a fire and kept us warm, and we listened to the radio. We listened to Nashville, Tennessee.

I was nearly grown before I was over in Huntsville except for just once a year at the picnic. When I was a child, they had a yearly picnic on the school hill, at that time in tall timber, and everybody looked forward to that the year round. It was a reunion where you saw all your kinfolks. That's where I met a lot of Mother's cousins I'd never seen. To go to Huntsville took all day on a horse, but we went in a wagon to the picnic. And we would get up real early and go, and it would be nearly noon when we got there. And we'd visit a while, and when we got back home it would be way after dark. That was one thing that Mother tried to see that we got to do. And the first airplane I ever saw on the ground had trouble and lighted in front of where we lived, and they stayed all night with us and got it fixed. They were making it to the reunion to show the airplane there. They tried to get Dad to let Mother and us kids ride in the airplane with them, and he said no. He was afraid they would have some more trouble. Back then there wasn't any place to stay, so if you had trouble, you stayed with people. We never locked a door and we never had anything stolen.

Maya Angelou

**b. 1928, Stamps, Lafayette County. Writer, actor, professor.
From *I Know Why the Caged Bird Sings*.**

The summer picnic fish fry in the clearing by the pond was the biggest outdoor event of the year. Everyone was there. All churches were represented, as well as the social groups (Elks, Eastern Star, Masons, Knights of Columbus, Daughters of Pythias), professional people (Negro teachers from Lafayette County) and all the excited children.

Musicians brought cigar-box guitars, harmonicas, juice harps, combs wrapped in tissue paper and even bathtub basses.

The amount and variety of foods would have found approval on the menu of a Roman epicure. Pans of fried chicken, covered with dishtowels, sat under benches next to a mountain of potato salad crammed with hard-boiled eggs. Whole rust-red sticks of bologna were clothed in cheese-cloth. Homemade pickles and chowchow, and baked country hams, aromatic with cloves and pineapples, vied for prominence. Our steady customers had ordered cold watermelons, so Bailey and I chugged the striped-green fruit into the Coca-Cola box and filled all the tubs with ice as well as the big black wash pot that Momma used to boil her laundry. Now they too lay sweating in the happy afternoon air.

The summer picnic gave ladies a chance to show off their baking hands. On the barbecue pit, chickens and spareribs sputtered in their own fat and a sauce whose recipe was guarded in the family like a scandalous affair. However, in the ecumenical light of the summer picnic every true baking artist could reveal her prize to the delight and criticism of the town. Orange sponge cakes and dark brown mounds dripping Hershey's chocolate stood layer to layer with ice-white coconuts and light brown caramels. Pound cakes sagged with their buttery weight and small children could no more resist licking the icings than their mothers could avoid slapping their sticky fingers.

Proven fishermen and weekend amateurs sat on the trunks of trees at the pond. They pulled the struggling bass and silver perch from the swift water. A rotating crew of young girls scaled and cleaned the catch and busy women in starched aprons salted and rolled the fish in corn meal, then dropped them in Dutch ovens trembling with boiling fat.

On one corner of the clearing a gospel group was rehearsing. Their harmony, packed as tight as sardines, floated over the music of the country singers and melted into the songs of the small children's ring games.

"Boys, don'chew let that ball fall on none of my cakes, you do and it'll be me on you."

"Yes, ma'am," and nothing changed. The boys continued hitting the tennis ball with pailings snatched from a fence and running holes in the ground, colliding with everyone. (133–35)

Fritz Hudson

b. 1929, Wells Bayou, near Dumas but in Lincoln County. Retired farmer. From notes written in 2010.

Everyone looked out for others. I remember one time a sharecropper came to Mother and told her of my racing a horse in the weeds where he knew there was a fallen log in the way. The horse jumped it and we kept running. He told her, "Lord God, Miss Emma, Watch that boy." People lived far apart and one way to get help if needed fast at night was to fire your shotgun rapidly three times and people knew you needed help.

We had a battery-powered radio and when Joe Louis fought it was put in a window and everybody came to listen. We had two mules with a fast fox trot that were loaned when people needed to get somewhere fast.

Gerald Bennett

**b. 1931, near Wesley in rural Madison County. Farmer.
Interview with Margaret Bolsterli, 1997.**

If a family got sick, they didn't have to worry about whether they were going to have plenty of wood or not or whether the cows would be milked because the neighbors would take care of that.

Billy Lee Riley

**b. 1933, Osceola, Mississippi County. Musician.
From Jeannie Whayne, "Interview with Billy Lee Riley,"
Arkansas Historical Quarterly (Autumn 1996)..**

My earliest memory is living in Osceola. Just being there and being a child there. I remember when I was like five years old, four or five years old, . . . I remember kids I used to play with. I remember we lived in a house that had black families on either side. And they had children our size and ages, and we just all blended in and played. There was no color barrier. That was on Red Row. That was where we lived. I remember when I was six or seven years old, there was two little black boys that I played with an awful lot, and we used to go downtown on Saturdays. Our families—and we would get separated from our families—[they] would take me around to the black section of town, and we would listen to the music. That was my first introduction to the blues. And it was just so, even at that young age, I knew that there was something there that I really did like. We would set around for hours and listen to that music coming out of the juke joints and maybe watch the guitar players sitting on the side of the street. . . . Those are memories that just linger and linger. . . .

I'm still living back there, I guess. That was such a good time for me. And I'm constantly comparing life today and life back then. Life today is such a fast life, such a competitive life. Everyone is competing. Everybody's got to have this. Everybody's got to have that. Back then nobody had anything. There were only two classes: the ones that had everything and those that didn't have anything. And it didn't bother us. We didn't care. The people we knew didn't have any more than we did, so we thought that's the way everybody lived. People loved each other. You could go to a neighbor's house, and if they had something, they'd give it to you. They wouldn't expect it back. (297–318)

LaVerne Williams Feaster

b. 1927, near Cotton Plant, rural Woodruff County. Retired state director of 4-H Clubs. Interview with Margaret Bolsterli, 2009.

I grew up near Cotton Plant, and the plantation we lived on was Big Dixie. That was our home out there until I was in high school when we moved to Cotton Plant. We had a wonderful community in Dixie. There was one church. It was a Baptist Church, and the people were all just like family. We would spend the night with each other and go to town with each other. It was just like everybody was everybody's family. I had two brothers. And they would go out in the woods and rivers and ditches and shoot marbles and play, but the girls had to stay home and play with dishes and dolls. But it was just like a community. If my mother had to go off, we'd go stay with somebody 'til she got back.

On the plantation at Dixie, we didn't have opportunities where we walked places, but when we moved to Cotton Plant, we would walk to the movies and down to the post office and the stores, and everybody knew what the rules were. And if you were not doing what you were supposed to do, whatever adult was there would correct you. And I never shall forget that I would be so glad when it would be raining or cold so nobody would be on the porches, because otherwise when I walked to the movies or store or whatever was going on and I would pass by Miss Crump's house, she would say "LaVerne, does your mother know that you've got your stockings rolled down?" Or if I had on a skirt, I would roll it up at the waistline to make it shorter. And before I could get back home, Mama would know that I had rolled up my dress. And they didn't have any telephone, and how they would get word to them was somebody would pass and Miss Crump would say, "You tell Miss Alma that I saw LaVerne pass here with her dress rolled." We knew what the rules were and what you were supposed to do.

William Grant Still

b. 1895, Little Rock. Composer, Musician. From "My Arkansas Boyhood," in *William Grant Still and the Fusion of Cultures in American Music* Robert Bartlett Haas, ed. .

What with all the propaganda being disseminated nowadays [1970], it may be hard for many people to believe that my boyhood was as it was—a typically American one, far removed from the ordinary concept of a little colored boy growing up in the South. I knew neither wealth nor poverty, for I lived in a comfortable middle-class home, with luxuries such as books, musical instruments and phonograph records in quantities found in few other homes of this sort.

All of this was the result of my having the good fortune to have been born to intelligent, forward-looking parents, as well as to the fact that Little Rock, where I grew up, was considered by many of us to be an enlightened community in the South. This was true to such an extent that in later years, when the city's name was splashed over headlines the length and breadth of the world, those of us who had lived there were amazed and incredulous. We could not believe that of Little Rock, because it was contrary to so much that we had known and experienced!

It is true that there was segregation in Little Rock during my boyhood, but my family lived in a mixed neighborhood and our friends were both white and colored. So were my playmates. In many instances, their friendship lasted over into adulthood. Stanley and Clifford, for example, were two little white boys who played with me. Their father was a friend of my stepfather. Boylike, we arranged an elaborate series of signals. We would have little flags or semaphores on our houses. These would be up when we were at home and down when we were away. This was so that we would not inconvenience our busy selves by calling on the others when the others were absent. When I returned to Little Rock, in 1927, after my mother's death, Stanley (who then lived in North Little Rock) came back to see me.

So, while I was aware of the fact that I was a Negro, and once in a while was reminded of it unpleasantly, I was generally conscious of it in a positive way, with a feeling of pride. At the same time, my association with people of both racial groups gave me the ability to conduct myself as a person among people instead of as an inferior among superiors. The fact that this could be done at all in the South represents, to me at least, an open-mindedness on the part of so many of the other residents of Little Rock. It would be completely unrealistic if I were to suggest that there were no incidents involving racial prejudice in Little Rock, because there were and they did make an impression on me. I even witnessed one such occurrence, which today would be termed "police brutality" on Center Street. It horrified me, but did not change my feeling that the good people of Little Rock overbalanced the bad. (75–76)

William H. Bowen

b. 1923, Altheimer, Jefferson County. Attorney, banker, university administrator. From *The Boy From Altheimer*.

Of course the school [Altheimer School] was for white students only. . . . In the Arkansas Delta and across the South, the prevailing viewpoint was, "Teach a black person to read and you lose a good cotton picker."

In 1939, I visited the Plum Bayou Township voting office in downtown Altheimer where my father was serving as a voting official during the election. I was there when Ed Freeman came to the door. He was my father's right-hand man and was a senior member of the team that operated the Altheimer Cotton Gin, and a senior carpenter in the crew that serviced the gin in the off-season, the cotton house, the cotton bale platform, tenant houses and other structures of the Elms Planting Company and the Bowen farm. On that day he motioned me to come to the door where he stood on the sidewalk. He asked to see my father and I asked him why he didn't just come in to the polling place. He said, "Oh no. Colored folks are not supposed to come in the voting places." The efforts to keep blacks from voting obviously worked in Altheimer. My father joined him on the sidewalk and they handled whatever business had necessitated the meeting, while the wall of disenfranchisement was left inviolate. (10–11)

Maya Angelou

At least twice yearly Momma would feel that as children we should have fresh meat included in our diets. We were then given money—pennies, nickels, and dimes entrusted to Bailey—and sent to town to buy liver. Since the whites had refrigerators, their butchers bought the meat from commercial slaughterhouses in Texarkana and sold it to the wealthy even in the peak of summer.

Crossing the Black area of Stamps which in childhood's narrow measure seemed a whole world, we were obliged by custom to stop and speak to every person we met, and Bailey felt constrained to spend a few minutes playing with each friend. There was a joy in going to town with money in our pockets (Bailey's pockets were as good as my own) and time on our hands. But the pleasure fled when we reached the white part of town. After we left Mr. Willie Williams' Do Drop

Inn, the last stop before whitefolksville, we had to cross the pond and adventure the railroad tracks. We were explorers walking without weapons into man-eating animals' territory.

In Stamps the segregation was so complete that most Black children didn't really, absolutely know what whites looked like. Other than that they were different, to be dreaded, and in that dread was included the hostility of the powerless against the powerful, the poor against the rich, the worker against the worked for and the ragged against the well dressed.

I remember never believing that whites were really real. . . . People were those who lived on my side of town. I didn't like them all, or, in fact, any of them very much, but they were people. These others, the strange pale creatures that lived in their alien unlife, weren't considered folks. They were whitefolks. (24–25)

Pearl Lou Mattmiller Katz

b. 1895, near Arkansas Post, rural Arkansas County. Taped account, 1985.

My oldest sister and the next five of us were brought into the world by the same black woman who had ushered my mother into the world. Her name was Harriet and we called her Aunt Harriet. That was a note of respect that we called elderly black people *aunt* because we would not have thought of calling her just Harriet. That would have been disrespectful. She was Aunt Harriet. When she passed on, Aunt Kitty was summoned. We had very loving, friendly relations with all the black people around us. We were, in a way, racists, I guess, because we thought that they had to be protected and taken care of because they didn't seem to have had the advantages that we had. And they didn't, at that time. They didn't. But they always found a ready response from my father if there was any trouble.

Joycelyn Elders

b. 1933, near Schaal, in rural Howard County.
Retired director of the Arkansas State Health Department;
Former U.S. surgeon general. Interview with Scott Lunsford,
Pryor Center, February 14, 2008.

You know, it's amazing. . . . This was our second move, I guess for me. And we lived in . . . a white farmer's old house, after he and their family moved away. And it was up the street, up the road, lane, from where his daughter lived. And they were really always very, very good to us. In fact, Miss May Dossy, they were the Dossys and the Joneses and she would, you know, when my mom would have a baby, I remember she would come up and wash. . . . That was back in the days when they thought you had to stay in the house for thirty days and stuff like that. Well, she would come up and do my mom's washing and help her cook and help to take care of us. And, well, you know, of course my mom . . . it was normal that she would go and work and help her. . . . And the most amazing thing, after I was here, not in this house, but after I became Health Director, she, I remember she was talking to somebody down in Nashville, and she was talking about me, and she said, "Oh, yes, I'm so proud of her. That's just one of my little nigger girls." . . . But you know, I didn't take it offensively. She was really meaning it very lovingly. She was very pleased that I had really done well and gone ahead and moved, and moved forward.

And I know my dad . . . he'd worked with a lot of the white farmers. . . . They had a kind of farmers' association or something, and they all couldn't buy . . . the hay cutters and the hay balers but they each would buy, get a piece. And they would all work together to cut and bale the hay and to try and get it in before . . . the rain. And I really don't ever remember our having any problem at all with the white community. . . .

Now we, you know, we knew we were black. They knew they were white. We knew our place and . . . we didn't try to go and get into their space. . . . We accepted it. Maybe we didn't have enough sense of ummph or whatever it takes to know better, but we accepted it. . . . It was never a pitting one against the other . . . so I don't remember us feeling, you know, we knew we were black people and they were the white people. . . . But I'm just saying that I don't remember it being any antagonism in this tiny community. And I've talked to my sisters and brothers . . . we've all talked about it. And we all agree, and even the woman who said "Well, that's my little nigger girl," well, her two daughters were teachers and they, when I was Health Director, they'd come up to see me. What I'm really saying is, we still, . . . really liked and respected each other, and if my mother had to have two dollars to send me to stay in college, she'd go over and they'd let her have the two dollars. But, and by the same token, if something happened and they needed my dad to come pull them out of the mud or do whatever, that just happened. . . . Everybody in the community would help one another as best they could. (25–27)

Sally Stockley Johnson

b. 1937, Marianna, Lee County. Retired teacher and Presbyterian minister. Interview with Margaret Bolsterli, 2009.

Black people were just part of the landscape and part of the structure of the community that worked in your house, took care of your yard. Just worked for people—they were just there. I never remember even questioning why we didn't go to school together until I was a junior in high school and *Brown vs. Board of Education* made us all aware that that was going to happen. And I remember that that was the first year I ever thought about all this on my own and thought that this is the right thing to do, these black children deserve a good education as much as I do. And I remember writing a theme called "The Talk of the Town" on which this wonderful teacher graded me off because he said it was a flippant title for a serious subject but he gave me an A. I was really proud of that.

My junior year was really important for me for several reasons. For one I thought about something on my own that went against what my parents thought; they definitely always taught us that black people were inferior. We were to be polite and courteous but never to socialize or anything like that. So, I knew that Mother and Daddy wouldn't agree with the thoughts I was writing down in this theme and it wasn't anything radical, but for a girl who had grown up in a very prejudiced, segregated South it was kind of unusual that I had these thoughts on my own. And it was the year my faith came to be important to me, on my own, and it was the year I decided I wanted to be a teacher. So it was an awakening year for me. And part of the reason was that the boy I had gone steady with had gone off to college, and I didn't have a boyfriend that year. So I began to establish who I was in my own mind as a person rather than somebody who was attached to a male, and that was important to me.

Daddy had always taught us to be fair. We hated to have him come out and play ball with us because he tried so hard to be fair to the other kids we felt he was unfair to his own. And I didn't know anything about what went on in the black schools, but it was obvious that they didn't have the same opportunities we had, and it just didn't seem fair. It just wasn't fair just because of the color of somebody's skin.

Grif Stockley

b. 1944, Marianna, Lee County. Attorney, writer. Brother of Sally Stockley Johnson. Interview with Margaret Bolsterli, 2009.

African Americans were everywhere on the streets and always deferential. You would go down Pearl Street where we lived and make a right on Alabama and it was gravel. There were black homes all along Alabama, and they were basically shacks, and that is where I would take the laundry. My big thrill when I was fourteen was getting to drive and take the laundry to Lula May. I would take a basket of laundry, and it seems like she got two dollars and fifty cents for this big basket of laundry. And she'd give me a basket and I'd take it home, and I'd drive like four blocks and come back onto Pearl Street, which was paved.

When I was in high school it was really upsetting when Sally [older sister] argued with Daddy [about race]. He was so important to me as a role model, that it's odd to talk about them [parents] because even though they were racist and white supremacist in their thinking, their ideal for me was: you have to tell the truth; you have to do your best. We had that drummed into us. He instilled in me a discipline that I still have today. As far as the racial consciousness, I don't think I got it 'til I was in college at Southwestern, and even though it was a conservative school, it was an idealistic time in the sixties. I always read the paper and stuff, and of course Kennedy was president. And we had Peace Corps recruiters come along, and of course they were kids who had just been in the Peace Corps and come back. And I can remember making, literally, a conscious decision, told myself I was going to make a million dollars or do something like the Peace Corps and do good. And I ended up going into the Peace Corps, and it was in the Peace Corps when I had to go off to Colombia, South America, to really be able to internalize poverty and injustice.

They [my parents] didn't use the N-word, and we were taught to be polite in that kind of paternalistic sort of way. They used *colored,* even *nigra* instead of *nigger.* That was not the same thing as saying *nigger.*

It was clearly white supremacy and racism, and Daddy was on the school board and voted, I'm sure, for stealing money from the black school. I have since done so much research on this. During the first days of the McMath administration there was an article on the front page of the *Arkansas Gazette* that Sid McMath's Department of Education revealed that there had been $4,250,000 diverted from black schools in the year 1948. They used the word *diverted* when in fact the new gymnasium in Marianna was coming out of funds that were supposed to be going to the black schools. Robert R. Moton, the black school, didn't have any of the amenities that we had. That was going on until there was a unitary school system in 1970 and it stopped.

Blacks knew not to get out of line or if they did they would be beaten by the police. There was just a lot of white privilege. We could go anywhere and know that if there was any kind of trouble, all Daddy had to do was call his best friend, Mr. Hal Mixon, who was the municipal judge, and we wouldn't get a speeding ticket or a parking ticket or anything like that. That part of the whole white supremacy was just understood; that's the way it was. Consciously you didn't think about that. You just somehow were able to exist in a way that you could have a senior play and do a minstrel, as we did, and not really think about it. I tell myself that I'm glad we weren't in blackface because it was so obvious and so basically cruel, but I'm sure if our sponsor had been asked, she would have said, "This is just good, clean fun." Even as close as we lived there was almost a conscious effort not to think about what the other was doing and how they existed and how things were for them.

Over at the black school then, there was a legendary black educator called Anna Strong who was principal, and she was very well respected. I remember hearing one of my relatives talk about how for some reason Anna Strong came to the front door of my aunt's house, and apparently they didn't have enough guts to tell her to go around to the back, like everybody else. They wouldn't go to the door themselves but sent their children, kind of as a way to put her in her place because she had such a strong personality that they had to treat her almost as if she were white but to let her know that they weren't going to come to the front door. Most African Americans in that time were so deferential and wouldn't look you in the eye. And of course they called me "Mr. Grif" as a ten-year-old. It's silly to say it was just segregation; it was white supremacy and it was enforced in so many different ways whether it was force, or threat of force, or theft of resources. And it went on and on and on.

Terry Shoffner

**b. 1947, Weldon, near Newport, Jackson County.
Artist and art professor. Interview with Margaret Bolsterli, 2009.**

When I look at it now, I think my family was really quite poor, but we were middle to upper class in that neighborhood. It was a largely black neighborhood, and I remember kids who were shoeless for the whole summer because they had one new pair of shoes for the year, and of course that was for school. They would play football barefooted in a sand burr patch and do as well as anybody else, which was always very strange.

There was a definite separation between the black and white kids. And we knew that we were different and we were separate, but it was our parents' point of view that these kids weren't the troublemakers. This was certainly a very racist neighborhood. And I am embarrassed to say this, but at the time I thought that I was better than they were. That was the prevailing attitude. There was a basketball hoop in my backyard, and I remember that there was a couple of black kids who would come down the alley and sit on the fence and wait until I invited them, and then they would come into the yard and we would play. Then the next morning, we would meet at the general store and often talk to one another although we were in different groups and then get on separate school buses to ride twelve miles to Newport to schools that were six blocks apart. This seemed perfectly normal. I graduated from high school in 1965; the schools were integrated in 1966.

One black kid in particular we knew as Tuffy. I never knew his real name, but he lived about four blocks away, and although this was not my core group of friends, I did mingle with them. I remember one time that as a member of the safety patrol at school I got to go to Memphis to be on a cartoon show, and I remember that my mother and dad invited Tuffy in to watch it on TV with them. That is the only time I can ever recall Tuffy being in my house.

Martha Conner McNair

**b. 1950. Lived near Augusta and later moved to
Newport, Jackson County. High school teacher.
Interview with Margaret Bolsterli, 2009.**

I have various memories of how different it was for us and black people. I remember when we lived in Newport, pretty early one morning, a knock came on the side door, and it was somebody who said that this woman who lived out on our farm had shot her husband point blank in his bed, that every morning she got up and went out and shot two squirrels and fixed them for him for his breakfast, but that morning she got up and shot him. That's the way it was put. He was, by all accounts, worthless and needed shooting. I figured that out later because there was no other accounting for this event. Daddy gave permission to bury him somewhere or permission to use this little church or a place to bury him on the farm or money to pay for digging the grave or whatever. They were taking her over into Oklahoma where she had Indian relatives. There was no trial; there was nothing. And I said, "Well, who are you reporting the death to?" and Daddy said, "Nobody," and I said, "Don't you have to get a death certificate," and he said "No, there's no birth certificate; all of that stuff just costs money." And I said, "Will there be any record anywhere?" And he said, "Well, on our books, there will." I said, "You mean like books for payment of wages," and he said "Yeah." And that was it.

I was in Memphis on the day Martin Luther King got shot. My mother and I were in the shoe department at Levy's. In those days you knew the people who worked in those department stores, or my mother did, and so this man came over and said, "Mrs. Conner you want to go on and get across the bridge. Something has happened and we don't know what it is, but you need to get across the bridge." So we got up and left right then. And then by the time we got home, which was about an hour from Memphis, it was on the news. The fires had started. My father was sitting there saying, "The northern media is going to come and . . ." He was a southern liberal, but I remember him saying that.

There was one black student in the class before me in 1966 and ten or twelve in my class in 1967. The father of the one in the class before me had more money and land than any of us, as far as we could tell. There was a little place called Blackville out near Auvergne, and her name was Willa Black. Her dad was named Pickens Black.

Jeannie Whayne

b. 1948, near Marked Tree, Poinsett County.
University professor. Interview with Margaret Bolsterli, 2009.

The civil rights stuff was confusing, but I think I was fortunate to have been raised during the civil rights movement. There was all this rhetoric flying around, and I think maybe it's natural for some kids to be questioning the values of their parents. But with the civil rights movement, you had an alternative narrative waiting there for you to articulate that was different from your parents'. As a kid in normal circumstances you might differ with your parents, but you don't have anybody giving you the cues, and you got that from the airwaves. Actually, Dorothy Stuck and her husband ran the newspaper there, and she wrote most of the editorials. And I read them and they were remarkably liberal and they had a significant influence on me. It made me significantly different from my family in terms of the civil rights movement. It made me look at what went on around me with different eyes. I also had my mother's first cousin who was very liberal and a very strong influence on me and my thinking about the fairness of the situation around me and looking at the poverty. I don't think I would have noticed that by myself. My parents didn't notice it; I wouldn't have got it from them. So I think it made me a different person from what I would have been if I had been raised a decade earlier. I wouldn't have had that same kind of awareness of the injustice. Even though, from my grandmother's point of view I was in a certain place in a social system and should be aware of where I was, those boundaries were not as well defined, from my point of view.

Randall C. Ferguson Jr.

b. 1951, Camden, Ouachita County. Business executive. Interview with Scott Lunsford, Pryor Center, March 28, 2006.

When I grew up, anybody could discipline you. . . . I mean, everyone understood what was expected of you. . . . Everybody had the same standards. There was no disagreement about what was right and wrong and how you should behave so you didn't have one person that tended to be more lenient than another. . . . So if we got out of line, it was everybody's job to get us back in line. Even if you were walking home from school and you were doing something, the neighbors would come outside and say, "Randall, Jr., you know you aren't supposed to be doing that." *Neighbors* would do that. And if we kept doing it, the phone rang at home and we were met by our parents when we got home. (13)

Karen Rudolph Shoffner

b. 1952, Fayetteville, Washington County. Financial advisor. Interview with Margaret Bolsterli, 2009.

By the time I was in the seventh grade all the black kids in Fayetteville my age were at the same junior high, all three of them. By the time I graduated from high school, in a class of 350 people, those same three were still in the class. We voted one of them a class officer. This was really thumbing our noses at Fayetteville at the time. We elected a black class officer! I didn't realize what racism in Arkansas was like until I went to east Arkansas at the age of seventeen and met my future in-laws and immediately got into huge rows with them. I had never been in an environment that tolerated the kind of racism they lived in everyday. There weren't any black kids in my class before seventh grade. But I do remember arguing with a kid who would run around the playground yelling "Two, four, six, eight, we don't want to integrate." I was horrified by that. That was not allowed in our house.

There was no antiblack prejudice; there was no racial language used. I suppose the black people I knew were from the university.

Sally Stockley Johnson

In Marianna there were town kids and country kids, and if the country kids were not common, you socialized with them. But if they were, they weren't invited to your birthday parties and later on you didn't date them or anything like that.

Billy Lee Riley

We always got a Sears catalog. The Sears catalog was the most welcome thing in our house because we called it the Wish Book. Everyone in those days called it the Wish Book. And we'd sit there every year and tally up everything we wanted before school was supposed to start. We would have it all down, man, and it never came true. I always wanted a mackinaw jacket, and my cousin always had a nice pair of lace-up boots. They was like logger boots. He always had a nice mackinaw and a nice cap. And I never had nothing, never had a coat, never had a pair of boots. That old catalog, though, it got its workout every year. We'd sit there and figure out what we was gonna have. "We're going to get it this year; we're going to get it this year." But we never did.

Sometimes we never had shoes. We only got shoes in the winter time. And they cost a dollar. The soles were glued on, and the first time we got kinda damp, got in a puddle of water, the soles of the shoes would come off. Dad used to put them back together with a little wire, wire them soles back on our shoes for us. . . . And a lot of times, that's why we didn't get to school. We didn't have clothes. We didn't have the lunches. They did have free lunches at some of the schools, and we did get some of that. But you go to school dressed like we had to dress and you were so humiliated by the ones that had more, that you just didn't want to go. My sister, that was exactly why she quit in fifth grade. She never would go back. And I only got three years of formal schooling. The reason I quit was I had to plow. (315–16)

Raymond Riggins

b. 1928, Texas. Grew up in Desha and Lincoln Counties near Dumas. Retired business executive. Interview with Margaret Bolsterli, 2009.

It would have been about 1943 when we moved in to Dumas. We had everything we needed, but we were poor. I had as nice clothes as anybody else. Nobody had a car, so it didn't matter that I didn't have one. My friends and I were the cream of the school. We were all the same, and it was wonderful. There was no difference between rich and poor, but most of them had more than I had. I wanted more than being a sharecropper, and from an early age I thought that I wanted my children to have more than I had, not necessarily material things but a better chance than my parents were able to give me. So I guess that it was an inner thing, and people that I associated with that gave me drive. I never felt that I was poor then. But I've told a story over the years that has got some laughs. Mama was walking down the middle of the street one night kicking a can, and as she passed Meadors drugstore Mr. Meadors came running out and said, "Mrs. Riggins, what in the world are you doing?" And she replied, "I'm moving."

Jerry Maulden

b. 1933, rural Cleburne County. Grew up in North Little Rock,
Pulaski County. Retired business executive.
Interview with Scott Lunsford, Pryor Center, 2007.

I'd say that the hurt I felt, as a kid, that I think gave me the drive that
I had to succeed was class differences. I mean, I had friends in high
school and junior high—well, even grade school—that lived in a different part of town—a much better part of town—difference in class.
And I would go home sometimes after school with those kids, and
the parents wouldn't let me in the house. In other words, it was kind
of like, "Well, you're from the wrong side of the tracks," you know?
And I learned—and I tell you—and I'm this way—I'm very kid ori-
ented. I really am. I mean I just love children. And I learned, that
adults just don't know how badly they can hurt a kid . . . with unkind
remarks, or rejection, because the kid and I were good friends—the
kids—more than one. And I would think, "What did I do?" But, anyway, you know, you're thinking, "What did I do?" I mean, I didn't
do anything. . . .

And so, maybe I didn't have the right clothes on. Maybe I didn't
dress as well as that son or something else. And I really believe it was
that rejection that put in me the desire, to succeed. . . . I had good
friends. I had really smart friends that made real good grades and
everything, but . . . And they're still good friends today, but that
instilled something in me. It was something to always overcome.
Someday I'll show them. Someday I'll show them.

A kind of a companion experience—North Hills Country Club—
I would go out there as a caddy. . . . Some of these uppity, uppity
businessmen out there at their nice country club—see, I've got a little
bitterness, playing golf—and they'd cuss me like I was a dog, you
know? . . . I mean, very profane—this, that, and whatever. I was doing
the best I could. I quit doing that, and I told people—and this is true:
. . . I feel more comfortable with the working-class, blue-collar people
than I feel with the country-club set. That's true. Even—even in a—
I've had to do what I had to do—it's business. But, you know, I know

real people when I see them. A lot of pretense at a certain level—a lot of pretense. . . . And I know—I know real people—common people are real people. . . . Blue-collar people are the salt of the earth. It's what makes America. . . .

When I became CEO of what then was the largest company in the state . . . on the top floor of the tallest building in this state—the day that I became CEO and was elected by the board, I was by myself late that night at the office. My office looked west and toward North Little Rock. And it was almost like a relief. I walked over—had my lights off so I could see the lights of North Little Rock. I walked over to the window, and I looked out over North Little Rock, and I said, "You didn't think I was worth anything? You thought I was nothing?" I talked to them. "You thought I was scum. Look at me now. Where are you? Look where I am, and you thought I was not worthy." Now that sounds childish, but I did it. And on the drive home that night . . . I thought, "That didn't really help me at all." It didn't do anything for me. You know what I'm saying? . . . People never know when they're unkind—particularly to young people—what kind of scars they can put in your heart. And I still resent those people today. And they're long gone. . . . But, I tell you this—they—they hurt a young man that . . . didn't deserve it. Now, this stuff is part of my interview. This is my deep feelings, and it's all of that background, that makes me a Democrat. (30–32)

Jeannie Whayne

I was the kid who didn't talk for six months because I had to train myself to speak correctly, in part because I hung out with other kids who didn't speak correctly. I remember having a moment of epiphany when I was about twelve or thirteen years old and I was sitting in my grandmother's drugstore, and a grandson of a friend of hers who was my age who was in town, home from boarding school, came in and sat down beside me. My grandmother always had this intense sense of class, and I didn't until I was around her, and then I was very much aware of class. He was very proper, a very nice little boy, but I realized that he could speak perfect English and I couldn't. And I sat there without saying a word because I was afraid I was going to embarrass myself and my grandmother if I said anything. And so that was sort of my moment of truth; on some level I felt I had to make a choice of what kind of future I was going to have. I can either go one way with my friends, or I can take my own route. My grandmother nagged about manners, and she may have nagged about grammar—I don't remember—but I was aware of it. I think it was that little boy.

So I got a little workbook to improve my vocabulary and would study it every night. At one point I got the idea, and I think I was right: I had imbibed too much vernacular language and so I didn't get my verb-noun agreement right in conversation. So I decided I was going to change that too. So I got some grammar books and read those. And then—it took me about six months, it seems to me—when I didn't say a whole lot in conversation with anybody because I had to consciously think about how I was going to say it so I would say it correctly because I didn't want to say it incorrectly. And it took a great effort of will to do that.

One of the things that is interesting to me is that intense class awareness or the differentiations that exist in small towns where a prac- titioner pharmacist could be so aware that she is better, that we are better than this other class of people. That we stand aside from them, that we don't associate with them. Of course I did, but I was aware that there were these differentiations and there were a number of them. My family was far from being at the top of the ladder; we were not big landowners, that was the top, nor bankers. My grandfather was a pharmacist, my father was a pharmacist and a gambler and we moved around all the time one step ahead of the bill collectors.

Shirley Abbott

b. Hot Springs but with roots in rural Garland County. Writer. From *Womenfolks*.

In a piece about Black English for the *New York Times*, James Baldwin observed that language is "the most vivid and crucial key to identity: it reveals the private identity and connects one with, or divorces one from the larger, public, or communal identity." My mother had such a language of identity—hillbilly English, which once was just such a key to identity as James Baldwin describes. The Southern migrant in the twentieth century has been forced to carry it around like a cardboard valise, evidence that he is a transient arriving in vain at the door of Grand Hotel. Hillbilly English was the language of the dying frontier, of the farm and the backwoods in an ancient social order. . . . It's wiry, leathery locutions come with a mythic overlay thrown in for free—poor white trash, mean and lowdown. Ignorant. Dumb. Like Black English, it causes doors to be slammed shut. This was my mother's speech, and it separated us. Women have carved identities distinct from their mothers' by having lovers or going to law school or getting married at dawn in their bare feet, but my ticket to independence was standard English.

. . . By the age of ten I had become a snob, as fearful of dangling my participles as of laying hold of the wrong fork at some well-set dinner table. Nobody north of the Mason-Dixon line would have been able to see much difference between my mother's manners and those of our city friends, but she was definitely an outsider. Furthermore, she knew she embarrassed me. I knew I was being an ass, even then, and I tried not to be embarrassed. . . . Between her and me there was much anguish. As any second-generation immigrant knows, to refuse to speak the language of one's ancestors is the ultimate breach. Yet she was able to forgive me one way or another for such tricks as going into the country with her and calling all the women "ahnt" instead of "aint." (162–65)

Dumas Bobcats in
1947 (Raymond
Riggins, #9; Fritz
Hudson, #5).
*Courtesy
Raymond Riggins*

African American Catholic-school children, Hot Springs. *Mary Hudgins Collection, MC 534, Box 99, Photograph 267, Special Collections, University of Arkansas Libraries, Fayetteville*

Apple Pickers at the Ras. B. Graham Orchard, Springdale (Washington County), about 1908. *Courtesy Shiloh Museum of Ozark History (S-68-19-99)*

Bill and Harriet Stockley and Tot. *Courtesy Sally Stockley Johnson*

Bill Covey, center, and friends. *Courtesy of Bill Covey*

Bonnie Brashears Pace, Combs (Madison County), Arkansas, 1994. *Katie McCoy, photographer. Courtesy Shiloh Museum of Ozark History (S-94-1-78)*

Boys playing on the Pea Ridge battlefield, 1969. *Author's collection*

Easter Sunday. Lillie Fears, top left. *Courtesy of Lily Fears*

Fannie Morgan and two children, Desha County 1895. *Courtesy of Virginia Sue Meade*

Gerald Bennett, 1941.
Courtesy of Gerald Bennett

Grif Stockley and Oliver Humphreys.
Courtesy Sally Stockley Johnson

Singing convention at the Good Luck School, Japton (Madison County), Arkansas, 1927. Leta Drake Parker, second from left, front row. *Courtesy Shiloh Museum of Ozark History/Walter Sizemore Collection (S-97-1-150)*

Harriet and Sally
Stockley, 1942.
*Courtesy Sally
Stockley Johnson*

Holly and Jennifer
Boone. *Courtesy
Holly Boone*

Haying scene, northwest Arkansas, 1900–1910. Courtesy Shiloh Museum of Ozark History (S-94-36-41)

Randall Ferguson as child, with two brothers James and Robert. *Ferguson 004.jpg, Drive 14, The David and Barbara Pryor Center for Arkansas Oral and Visual History, University of Arkansas, Fayetteville*

Jeannie Cazort and Cecile Cazort Zorach. *Courtesy Cecile Cazort Zorach*

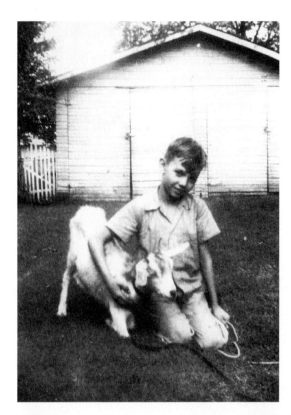

Jerry Maulden as child, with goat. *Jerry Maulden with goat-1.tif, Drive 19A, The David and Barbara Pryor Center for Arkansas Oral and Visual History, University of Arkansas, Fayetteville*

Karen Rudolph Shoffner and B. A. Rudolph in carriage. *Courtesy Carol Rudolph*

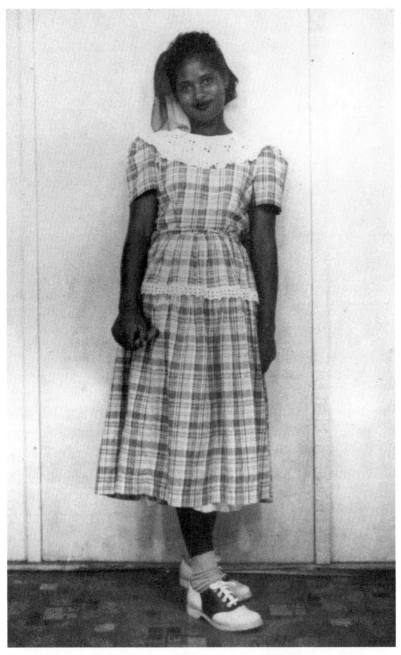

Joycelyn Elders in high school in Tollette, Arkansas. *04EldersJoycelyn.tif, Drive 19A, The David and Barbara Pryor Center for Arkansas Oral and Visual History, University of Arkansas, Fayetteville*

Julie Gabel.
*Courtesy of
Julie Gabel*

Karen Rudolph
Shoffner and Butch
Rudolph ready for
the party. *Courtesy
Carol Rudolph*

Kenneth Rex Jones and hogs. *Dorothy Core Collection. MC 1380, Box 86-9, Photograph 293, Special Collections, University of Arkansas Libraries, Fayetteville*

LaVerne Feaster and her first car. *Courtesy LaVerne Feaster*

Langston High Twirlers on parade, Hot Springs. *Mary Hudgens Collection. MC 534, Box 99, Photograph 293, Special Collections, University of Arkansas Libraries, Fayetteville*

Madelyn and Dorothy Jones with bullfrog. *Dorothy Core Collection. MC 1380, Box 86-6, Photograph 273. Special Collections, University of Arkansas Libraries, Fayetteville*

Mary Elsie Robertson in her soldier suit during WWII. *Courtesy Mary Elsie Robertson*

Michael Thomas.
Courtesy Michael Thomas

CHAPTER 2

Family and Memory

Memories of family frequently begin with the dinner table and the food on it, often lovingly described for its variety, provenance, and methods of preparation. It is worth noting that people who grew up poor during the Depression but had enough to eat are careful to mention this. Everyone knew of families where children went to bed hungry. In considering the different levels of poverty, a hungry family was at the terrifying bottom of the list.

The table was the center of family life where manners were taught, children reprimanded, and matters of interest discussed. It was the place where parents expected to have their children's attention and took pains to make sure they had it. After supper, during the school year, it was the place for homework, frequently under close parental supervision. When school was not in session, the table was still the center in early years, because in rural areas, before electricity, it was the place where the kerosene lamp stood. Reading in the evening after supper was a common family entertainment, with the mother or father reading aloud for all the children to listen. Since reading material was scarce, people remember reading whatever they could get their hands on. In many families before radio and television, parents and children sang together and sometimes played instruments; many sang together in the house and in the fields as they worked.

Parents and children usually spent a great deal of time together whether playing or working. Boys hunted and fished with their fathers, and girls did whatever their mothers were doing.

Church was a family affair, and everyone able to walk was expected to go. It sometimes provided activities all day Sunday and Wednesday nights as well, and revival meetings held in the summer were anticipated and reveled in by most denominations. Balanced against the pleasure of taking part in the church activities and the promise of joy to come, the threat of damnation was a source of terror never to be forgotten by many children.

Pearl Lou Mattmiller Katz

Our home was about three miles north of Arkansas Post and six miles east and south of Gillett. Arkansas Post was a village of twelve or fifteen families at that time and had two stores and one doctor, Dr. Hudson, and these stores were furnished their merchandise by boats that came up the Arkansas River. Gillett had a bank and railroad station and an ice house. It had two Methodist churches—a north Methodist church and a south Methodist church. There may have been a Catholic church and later on there was a Lutheran.

Our home was between those two villages. It was a four room house: a large room and a small room on each side of a wide hallway. . . . In 1900 my father engaged the services of my uncle to build an ell on that house with four more rooms, two upstairs and two down.

The dining room and kitchen were on one side of the hall, and my mother's bedroom on the other side of the hall was our sitting room most of the year. And in another little bedroom by hers, in the same bed, all eight of her children were born. The midwives charged three dollars! The children did not have special beds or cribs or special rooms to go to. The babies slept between their parents until they were at least a year old and probably more. The babies usually stayed in their parents' bed until another one came, usually about two years apart, and so they would have at least fifteen months with their parents. So they had that tender, warm love all the time because their parents were right there so their little hands could touch their warm flesh. They never had a sense of being alone or abandoned or short changed of their mother-love or their father-love because they slept right there between them.

When we were children, we read and read, and let me tell you something funny. Our mother and father's bedroom had some canvas, almost like cheesecloth, stretched on it and tacked on the walls. We had the walls papered then with old copies of the *Dewitt New Era* newspaper. It wasn't pretty, but it was very efficient, and I learned to read before I ever went to school by reading the newspaper tacked on the walls. Now very few people have ever had the opportunity to do that kind of thing.

Our mother read to us a lot, and there is something I remember learning: "Richer than I he can never be for I had a mother who read to me." We had a mother who read to us and fostered in us the desire to read and the ability to read. In winter we would lie on the floor with our feet towards the fire and listen to our mother read. And our daddy would be there too reading the paper or the Bible. We were all taught to read the Bible, and we had Bible stories that we read avidly. And we read books, books, and books.

When we were children and sitting around our dining room table after supper studying our lessons, our mother saw to it that we got those lessons. She would ask us questions on the lessons to see just how much we had studied so we were early taught to apply ourselves.

William Grant Still

In shaping my attitudes, my mother had a most important role to play. She was constantly "molding my character," trying to keep me from "following the path of least resistance," impressing on me the fact that I *must* amount to something in the world. (it never occurred to her or to me that any other course was possible, even though she and I had different ideas as to the means of accomplishing it), correcting my grammar and my accent, and never sparing the rod lest her child be spoiled. (76)

Leta Drake Parker

There was a mill over on Lollar Creek and a store with the post office at Draketown. Granddad had a fine saddle horse, and he would ride over there to get the mail and get his wheat ground.

We had a garden with everything there was to eat in it. We grew a big enough garden. We grew enough potatoes to do us 'til potatoes came in again; we canned everything we could can. We bleached apples, where you tie them in a sack and put a pole across a barrel and put that sack across that pole and let the apples be down in each end of the sack and you take a big pan of coals and set it down in the bottom of that barrel and put sulfur on it and cover it up. They call them bleached apples. You put them in a fruit jar and put a lid on them. They're quartered up. And you take them out and fry them and they are delicious, especially when you haven't had any raw fruit in a long time. Of course we dried peaches. We had two window screens, and we'd lay little freestone peaches between them. My mother wouldn't leave them out in the flies like other people did. For sweet potatoes, to save them, we wrapped each potato in a SearsRoebuck catalog leaf and put it in a wooden box and set it in the living room pretty close to the fireplace. We had a fire in the fireplace pretty near all the time, and we had a Dutch oven. We would put on some coals and put some paper in there and wash the sweet potatoes and put them in and another paper over them, lay the lid on, and shovel coals on that, and there is nothing that smelled any better nor tasted better than those potatoes. And my granny made cornbread that way a lot of the times. We had a wood cookstove. We had kerosene lamps, and my mother shined them just about every day to keep the globes clean where we could see.

When I was little, all we bought at the store was kerosene and matches and just a few other things. Bought sugar but mostly we had molasses. Raised our own hogs. I was raised on pork; I didn't know what beef was. We kept a few hens and had chickens and eggs to eat and a few eggs to sell to buy the kerosene and things. We had hens that laid under the barn, and I'd crawl under there and get the eggs, and we'd take them to town and get some money. We had milk and butter. We just had to live at home. We hardly had any money, and any money we got went for necessities. I was nearly grown before I saw any kind of [store-bought] soap. We had an ash hopper and saved our ashes all year. And in the spring we carried water and poured in there and made lye to make soap, and that would clean anything because it was nearly all lye. The thickness of it was clabbered, sort of like a beat-up jello. In our yard we had a lilac and a rosebush, but you didn't have other kinds of flowers back then. They used asparagus for beauty spots in the yards.

My mother taught me to be saving. We patched everything that got a hole in it, and I still do.

Gerald Bennett

The biggest difference I can see in families now and when I was small is the lack of communication now. The whole family is seldom at home at the same time. People don't sit down together at the table and talk. Now I was the baby, and when I was little, I couldn't sleep until all my brothers and sisters got home at night. I'd lie there and worry until the last one was home.

The average twelve-year-old child now has more money than most anybody had sixty years ago. The money just wasn't there. They had these little old movies came around, and it was a dime apiece for a child to get in. There was so little to do that people would go watch them even if there was no sound system. I never did see one of them. My dad always had the money for us to go, but he would have to scratch the bottom out of his pocket to get it. I had five sisters and three brothers. I never did realize we were poor. I know now that we were but none of us ever went hungry. We always had clothes to wear.

My mother would can four or five hundred jars, she called it. Some of them might be half gallons, very few pints. It was a big family so pints weren't worth canning, so it would be quarts or half gallons. And she would put up sometimes seven hundred and fifty or a thousand jars of that. For a long time, up until 1938 or so she put them upstairs wrapped with quilts and everything else to keep them from freezing. And there was some of the best food up there you ever saw. She'd can sausage as well as vegetables and fruit. Back then you could pick all the grapes that you wanted, wild, which have ten percent better flavor than tame. She'd pick those, blackberries, dewberries, wild strawberries. We'd drink blackberry juice, dewberry juice, grape juice. I don't live that good anymore. Always had cows and laying hens. My mother was a good hand with a hen. I'd bet seventy percent of what we bought in a grocery store was paid for with eggs from a hen. Either that or cream. She had sixty or seventy hens. Had all the milk and butter we wanted. We killed lots of hogs, grew sorghum. There was a mill in the community and the guys running the mill made the molasses on shares. If I ever went to bed hungry, I don't remember it, but there were children my age right here in this neighborhood that did.

People had fun back then. After the day's work was over you didn't have such stress.

Phydella Hogan

b. 1918, rural Washington County. Retired music store owner. Interview with Margaret Bolsterli, 1997.

I was raised out at Zion, five and a half miles from Springdale and seven and a half from Fayetteville. There were three boys and three girls and I was third from the last.

We raised most of our food, did lots of canning and drying, and we killed our own hogs for meat. We seldom had beef, unless, sometimes, there'd be a calf, and we'd have a little veal. But the hog, you could salt that down and have the hams and stuff like that. We had our own cow, one horse to plow with, and we didn't have enough land. There was only five and a half acres. But we managed to get by pretty good. We never went completely hungry. A lot of times we didn't have enough clothes. It was hard to get shoes and things for school.

We talked at the table. Quarreling at the table was not allowed, and everybody came to the table at the same time. If Mother or Dad told any of us to hush, we didn't need a second warning. Usually at six in the morning we had breakfast, on the dot of twelve we had dinner, and then about six or six thirty of an evening was suppertime and we ate what was left over from dinner. I was always reading, and once I took a book to the table and was told to put it away. I could read when I got through.

I can't remember learning to read. I know I was reading before I was five, and I can't remember learning to sing, either. And oh, we sang all the time. And it was all by ear because none of us except Mother and Dad could read a note. They read shape notes and had beautiful voices. They didn't join in with us very often, but when they did, oh boy, we loved it. Mother sang all the time. Every job she was doing, no matter where she was in the house when you got home from school, you knew where she was 'cause you could hear her easy, singing or humming. That's where I learned so many old folk songs and gospel songs. Mother sang gospel. Dad didn't sing unless he was just having fun with us kids or went to church. But he had a beautiful voice. Mother must have had a little bit of voice training. She had that little quiver in her voice.

When I was just turning six, my sister Helen was three years younger and just starting to talk, but she could sing, could carry a tune at two. There was a post office and general store right next to our house at Haberton, and Mother would let us go there because we didn't have to cross the road. We could go there and pick up the mail. If somebody heard us singing outside, 'cause we sang all the time, they'd ask us to sing. There were usually a few old men sitting around, like they do, and the storekeeper and they'd all give us a penny's worth. We were always anxious to go get the mail! And Mother noticed that we were not eating our meals and stopped the supply of candy for us.

We made our own plays. My older sister used to write little plays we'd perform. We were big hams.

Robert E. Jones

b. 1926, near Watson, Desha County. Retired merchant. Self-taped recollections, 2010.

During my childhood there was a lot of talk about the 1927 flood. They talked about things before the flood as if that were a romantic era that had things we didn't have when I was a child, such as a radio. Also, when I was in early childhood, there were no churches in Watson. They had all been destroyed by the flood. We had church and Sunday school upstairs in the high school, and they ran the school bus on Sunday so anybody could go to church and Sunday school that wanted to. It wasn't unusual for the Methodist preacher to come spend Saturday night at our house.

There's a difference in the way things are done now when people die. Our family cemetery is about a quarter of a mile from the house, and in the summer of 1931, when I was five, my brother Paul died, and I still remember his casket being carried to the cemetery on a T-model Ford truck owned by a bootlegger who made the remark that he couldn't understand why a young person like that was taken in death and someone like him was left to live. When I was eleven or twelve, my aunt Sallie died, and her funeral was held at the house too, and the casket was carried to the cemetery in a wagon pulled by mules. Neighbors and family came and sat with those caskets night and day until the burial. But when our mother died in 1953, it was a shock to me that her body was left at the funeral home and no one was sitting with her. That had changed from the time that Aunt Sallie died in 1936. By then, funeral homes took care of situations that the neighbors used to take care of.

And I remember that with everybody, every child I went to school with, there was a death in the family, and the school superintendent would let anyone go to the funeral who wanted to and would run a school bus to the cemetery to take them there.

I remember being in the garden, in the potato patch with Mother, when she was bitten by a snake. The Chidesters were living just up the road, and Mother started running there. And I tried to keep up with her, and she ran off and left me. And Mrs. Chidester grabbed up a chicken, ripped it open alive, and stuck Mother's hand in there for the warmth to draw the poison out. I don't recall how we got there, but then we went to Watson, to the school, to get my brothers and sister because so often a snake bite was fatal.

There were no churches out in the country, and some of the people would build brush arbors out of four willow poles with the limbs, leaves, and branches put over the top. And the benches would be logs, and they would have their meetings there. Revivals usually started after cotton chopping and before cotton picking started. We called them *holy rollers*.

Billy Lee Riley

There was a time there, for about a year, that we did fairly well. . . . I think it was somewhere near 1941, 1942. The best I can remember. I know I was real small, but I do remember the money. I remember we got to go to the movies more, and we had a little more to eat. But most of the time, very little food is really not the word. There was no food. There was a many a time that we went to bed without, maybe we hadn't had anything to speak of all day. My mother would cry at night, and we didn't know what she was crying about. But we could hear her in the other room and she was crying for us. She was crying because we were hungry and there was no way to get any food. She would go out and find this wild salad, the edible kind, and cook that and that would be our food for the day. Beans and potatoes and stuff like that was luxuries. To set down to a breakfast like we do now, bacon and eggs, or something like that was a big treat. But if Dad was working, we always knew on Friday night we would have either, as Barney Fife calls it, a pounded steak or pork chops, lettuce and sliced tomatoes. . . . And the next day we went to town to the movies and Monday morning it was back to worrying again.

We ate anything that was edible. When I was a child, the city dump was right over on the levee in Osceola from us, and people was so hungry at that time that there used to be big fist fights at the city dump over who was going to get what the city was dumping out. And sometimes there was things you could eat, you could take it home and clean it. If the bread had mold on it, you cut it off, and fruit that had mold you just cut it and cleaned it up. When you're in that predicament you know what to do. It's either that or starve. Many of our meals came out of that city dump. It wasn't the bad stuff. We would never eat nothing like that. It was what they threw away at grocery stores, restaurants. To us that was great food. We weren't the only ones. I don't want you to think we were the only ones sitting there hungry. Everybody in that area, Red Row and Rag Row, we were fighting to live, fighting to survive. I call it the good old days, and I still do, and I'm going to tell you even though it was bad, I would still go back rather than live in the future I'm afraid we're going to have. For one thing, the people cared. (314)

Joy Nuckols Hudson

**b. 1930, Dumas, Desha County. Retired high school teacher.
From handwritten notes, 2009.**

From kerosene lamps to cyberspace—more advances in technology in my lifetime than at any other time in the history of this planet.

I lived on a farm until I was four—I can remember my parents reading by kerosene lamps—and my mother heating a big cast iron pot outdoors to wash clothes and rubbing them on a corrugated washboard. I think we had a battery operated radio because we didn't have electricity. When my Grandfather Burrus visited, he would sit on the porch with me on his knee and play his harmonica.

. . . We moved to town [Dumas] when I was four and at that time there were only four children in our family. In town we had electricity. I remember vividly our first electric washing machine—it was basically a big white tub with an agitator with 2 rollers to push the clothes through to wring them out. My mother still cooked on a big cast iron wood stove; she was an amazing cook, turning out three hot meals a day with at least two pies or a cake at lunch and supper, as our night meal was always called. . . . Then there were two more little ones, making six children in all.

. . . We always ate every meal as a family and my Dad always made sure that our manners were impeccable. No shenanigans and no arms on the table. After supper, we usually sat around the table and listened to the radio—great comedy programs like *Baby Snooks, Jack Benny, Fibber McGee and Molly, Fred Allen, The Shadow, The Green Hornet, The Hit Parade, Red Skelton, Jack Armstrong, The Lone Ranger*, etc. *Stella Dallas* was a daytime serial but my mother never had time to listen to it.

Johnny Cash

b. 1932, Kingsland, grew up at Dyess, rural Mississippi County. Musician. From *Cash: The Autobiography*, with Patrick Carr.

Inside me, my boyhood feels so close, but when I look around, it sometimes seems to belong to a vanished world. In the United States in the late 1990's, is it really possible to imagine whole families, boys and girls of eight to eighteen at their parents' sides in the cotton fields, working through the July heat from dawn to dusk, driving away exhaustion with songs of the spirit? Are there still places where a young boy can leave his house after breakfast with just a fishing pole and spend the whole day rambling and adventuring alone, unsupervised and unafraid, trusted and un-feared for?

Perhaps there are, I hope so. But I suspect otherwise. I suspect that if such places do exist, our televisions have blinded us to them.

. . . The first song I remember singing was "I Am Bound for the Promised Land." I was in the back of a flatbed truck on the road to Dyess, Arkansas, from the first house I remember living in: the place next to the tracks out in the woods near Kingsland, Arkansas, where my family had ended up after a succession of moves dictated by the rigors of the Depression. That was a real bare-bones kind of place, three rooms in a row, the classic shotgun shack.

. . . The new house toward which the flatbed truck was taking us was something else, a brand new deal of the New Deal. Late in 1934, Daddy had heard about a new program run by the Federal Emergency Relief Administration in which farmers like him who had been ruined by the depression were to be resettled on land the government had bought. As he explained it in later years, "We heard that we could buy twenty acres of land with no money down, and a house and barn, and they would give us a mule and a cow and furnish groceries through the first year until we had a crop and could pay it back, and we didn't have to pay until the crops came in." That's exactly what the deal was, and more: in forty-six different places in the agricultural United States, these "colonies" were being created on a cooperative basis. In the settlement toward which we were headed, we and all the other families would have a stake in the general store, the cannery, the cotton gin and other facilities; we were all responsible for them and we all shared in their profits, if any. The cotton we produced would go into the communal crop to be sold higher up the line for better prices than small individual crops could be. So as I've said in the past, I grew up under socialism—kind of. Maybe a better word would be communalism.

. . . . I remember coming to that new house so clearly. It took us two days to travel the 250 miles from Kingsland, first on gravel roads and then on dirt roads turned to mud by a hard, bitterly cold rain. We had to stop overnight by the roadside in the truck the government had sent for us and we kids slept in the back with just a tarpaulin between us and the rain, listening to Moma cry and sing.

. . . When we finally got to Dyess, the truck couldn't get up the dirt road to our house, so Daddy had to carry me on his back the last hundred yards through the thick black Arkansas mud—gumbo, we called it. And that's where I was when I saw the Promised Land: a brand new house with two big bedrooms, a living room, a dining room, a kitchen, a front porch and a back porch, an outside toilet, a barn, a chicken house, *and* a smokehouse. To me, luxuries untold. There was no running water, of course and no electricity; none of us even dreamed of miracles like that.

. . . Moma inherited Grandfather Rivers's talent and his love for music. She could play guitar, and fiddle too, and she sang well. The first singing I remember was hers, and the first song I remember myself singing was one of the songs of faith she'd learned as a child. I was about four years old, sitting in a chair right beside her on the front porch. She'd sing, "What would you give"—and I'd chime right in with my part, continuing the line—"in exchange for your soul?"

We sang in the house, on the porch, everywhere. Daddy would be by himself, plowing, and we kids would be with Moma, chopping cotton and singing. I'd start it off with pop songs I'd heard on the radio and my sister Louise and I would challenge each other: "Bet you don't know this one!" Usually I knew them and I'd join in well before she finished. Later in the day, we'd all sing together, hillbilly songs and novelty songs, what ever was going round at the time . . . and then, as the sun got halfway down toward the west and our spirits started flagging, we'd switch to gospel: first the rousing up-tempo songs to keep us going, then, as the sun began to set, the slower spirituals... We closed each day in the fields with "Life's Evening Sun is Sinking Low."

. . . I bet [modern farmers] also have some of the same great pleasures that lit up my young life. When the cotton began to open in October, for instance, it was just beautiful. First, there'd be lovely white blooms, and then, in about three days they'd turn to pink, whole fields of them. What a picture that was.

That wasn't all, either, under those pink blooms there'd be tiny, tender little bolls, and they were such a sweet treat. I used to pull them off and eat them while they were still tender like that, before they began turning fibrous, and I loved them. My mother kept telling me, "Don't eat that cotton. It'll give you a bellyache." But I don't remember any bellyache. I remember that taste. How sweet it was! (12–21, 52–53)

Raymond Riggins

I was five years old when we came to Watson and homesteaded ground on Cypress Creek. We went back to Texas when I was seven and returned to Arkansas to Cypress Creek when I was eleven years old. My father and brother came first with horses and equipment and built a house. Then the rest of us came on the train, and all our furniture and things were loaded on a wagon for the trip to Cypress Creek. The wagon got stuck in the mud, and the horses pulled it in two, and everything we had fell into the mud. I remember my mother crying because everything we had was in the mud and our only source of transportation was pulled in two in the middle of it. The wagon had to be taken out and repaired. That took a day or two, and we walked on in another three or four miles and across the creek on the walk log.

We always had plenty of food and some money from the crops, and mother raised a big yard of chickens. Always had a calf or hogs to butcher, and the woods were full of animals like squirrels, raccoons, rabbits, and every kind of an edible animal you could think of. And we hunted them, not for sport but for the groceries. We always had settings of chickens in the spring. And when the chickens got big enough so you could tell the hens from the roosters, mama would save the hens for laying eggs, and then we would start killing off the older hens, and Mama would bake those. It was my job to run the chicken down and kill it. She would say, "Get one of those roosters," and I would wring its neck. We had guineas that were like watchdogs; if any animals like panthers or foxes were to come up to the chicken house or get after the calf or pigs, those guineas would raise Cain, day or night.

We had every kind of animal and reptile in the world. Somebody had given me a little duck for Easter, and I was so proud of that duck.

It would follow me around and everything, and we had a bell at the back of the house for emergencies. One day Mama heard a rattlesnake and thought it was in the house so she rang the bell, but my brother got there and didn't find it in the house and looked under the house. And there the rattlesnake was, and it had eaten my little duck.

Joycelyn Elders

We didn't have electricity for a long number of years. . . . We had kerosene lamps for lighting the house and for studying. In fact for most of the time until I was probably in the sixth or seventh grade or maybe later than that—in order to study or read—I loved to read. We didn't have much to read, but I would get under the quilts, you know? Under—get a quilt and put over—and put the lamp under the quilt. I think of how dangerous that is now, but, you know, to keep warm . . . if it was at night. The only place we had a heater . . . was the—the fireplace. So my mom and dad was in this one big room where they had the fireplace . . . and the rest of us were . . . in this one little room. You know, there was obviously no insulation. Sometimes windows were broken. You had cardboard over the windows. . . . This is the second house that I am really talking about. The very first house . . . we had kind of this one big room with a fireplace. Then we had a kitchen, and then we had one other little, you know, shack appendage attached onto that room. And that was our home.

. . . I forget how many aunts and uncles I had, but many. But every Sunday I remember we used to—my dad would hook up the wagon and we would get in the wagon and it was probably five or six miles from where my grandparents lived and where my parents in their farm shack was living, and we would drive up the country roads and through the woods and past the church and up to that—my grandparents house. It would be a super country shack by our style today, but they were really—we thought, that where they lived was so much better than where we lived. You know, they had, I think—

probably five or six rooms and they had a—a hallway. . . . You know, a large hall . . . the big front porch and then you had the hall that went through the length of the house so—to keep it cool. . . . And so my grandmother always had a huge Sunday dinner, and it was just—and all of my aunts and uncles were always there and—you know, to me it was just a wonderful outing on Sunday, and that is where we always went on Sunday. . . . That's just what you did. Nobody ever thought of doing anything else.

. . . We used the home remedies, the quinine and the asafetida, castor oil and kerosene on sugar cubes. . . . I remember, again, very early, my brother got very ill and . . . usually when we got ill, with diarrhea or something or stomach ache, well, we *all* got ill. But just my brother this time was ill. And I remember his abdomen became very distended and he was very sick. And I remember my mom telling my dad, "Curtis, you're gonna have to take my baby to the doctor." And my dad had made some kind of little rig, saddled it up, and put it on the horse . . . to take my brother to the doctor. Well, when he got there . . . the doctor put in a drainage tube, to drain out the pus and sent him back home. But that was all, you know, they didn't have any place to hospitalize black children. So . . . when you got sick, you went to the doctor's office and you waited all day until all the white patients were seen and then he would see the black patients. And so when he got to my brother he said the only thing he could do is open it, and I remember now, it was a big red tube hanging out of my brother's abdomen when he came back home. But can you imagine going thirteen miles on the back of a mule, how awful that must've [been] and then back home? My brother lived and became a veterinarian. I say he was treated like a pig, so he learned to take care. (5–40)

Jerry Maulden

I was born outside of Shirley, Arkansas. And if you're on the road from Shirley to Heber Springs—there comes a forks of the road, and one fork to the left goes to Heber, and the other goes to now what is . . . the lake.

. . . My first memory was sitting in my dad's lap, and he had a Sears catalog, and he was showing me things in there, and I must've been three. And I remember this. Why, I don't know. Traffic light. He was telling me about what a traffic light was. And I thought, "Wow." You know, I'm a little country kid at this stage.

My dad and I were pretty close, and the most vivid of the memories of living there was he had worked for the WPA [Works Progress Administration], and he was so proud of that later because when we would be back up in that part of the country where our relatives were, he would point out a culvert, and he'd say, "Jerry, I put that—I helped put that culvert in. I helped build that bridge." And back then, you know, I mean, the people were so proud of the work they did for what they got. And I'll be honest, that was the beginning of my becoming a Democrat . . . because of that. But, you know, the WPA program ended, and he had worked in sawmills and that sort of thing, but that work went away. And so he had to leave to come to Little Rock—to North Little Rock is where he ended up, to find work. And I remember that in our car—my older brother, my mother, and me and my dad, drove to Clinton. And he got in the back of a pickup truck with several other men, and I just think about this—and all of them in the same boat— they need work. They need to earn money for their family, and they were going to Little Rock to search for work. And I remembered just— I was traumatized. I was crying and crying and traumatized. And my dad was trying to tell me before he got in the truck, and my mom, that, "He'll be back. He'll be back." But that—that memory played, I think, an important role in my future and the way I felt about things. . . . I mean, it's just the— the fact that for a man—I can't think of anything worse than for a man with a family to want a job, to need a job, to love his family—the hurt he must feel in not being able to provide. And that, you know—that was something that stayed with me—has stayed with me the rest of my life. (2–3)

Levon Helm

b. 1940, rural Phillips County near Marvell. Musician, actor.

From *This Wheel's On Fire*, with Stephen Davis. I was born in the house my father rented on a cotton farm in the Mississippi Delta, near Elaine, Arkansas. . . . I'm talking about a low, flat water world of bayous, creeks, levees, and dikes, and some of the best agricultural land in the world for growing cotton, rice and soybeans. . . . Think of endless cotton fields, gravel roads, groves of pecan trees, canebrakes, bayous, pump houses, kudzu vines, sharecroppers' cabins, tenant farmhouses, flooded rice fields, the biggest sky in the world, and the nearby Mississippi, like an inland sea with its own weather system. Think 110 degrees in the shade in the summer time. Cotton country. We were cotton farmers.

. . . Don't even think about electricity. We might have used a battery-powered radio until I was ten years old. . . . If I think back, I can still hear faint echoes of "Blue Moon of Kentucky" on our family radio. We'd have to buy a battery two and a half feet long and maybe eight inches thick; a big heavy damn thing! I remember our dad pulling our tractor right up to the window of the house one night when the battery was down, and he plugged the radio into the tractor battery so we wouldn't lose *The Grand Ole Opry, The Shadow, The Creaking Door, Amos 'n Andy*—those were the shows you couldn't miss. *Sky King.* From about four-thirty in the afternoon on, I was so close to that radio that my memories are of the rest of the family behind me. That was our entertainment. My dad and Clyde Cavette would go to town and get two fifty-pound ice blocks that would fit in our iceboxes. You could chip off them for a week. They'd buy an extra fifty pounds of ice, and we'd get together that night and make freezers of ice cream. Mom and Arlena would bake up a couple of big cakes, one coconut, one pecan. On special occasions the two moms would collaborate on lemon icebox pies, their own invention. They'd beat two cans of Pet milk until it was whipped to foam, adding sugar and lemon juice until it congealed. Then they'd freeze it in the icebox. I loved this beyond belief. It was so sweet your mouth would pucker. After I was old enough to work, they'd have to make three pies; one for each family and one for Lavon. And I'd *guard* mine. Then we'd make the radio the main feature, maybe play cards, visit.

. . . We were a musical family. Mama sang in a clear alto voice and Dad and I sang together as far back as I can remember. He liked all kinds of music and taught me "Sitting on Top of the World" when I was four years old. . . . Going to music shows was high-level entertainment for our family. They'd set up tents at the edge of Marvell and have a stage, folding chairs, and refreshments. The first show I remember was Bill Monroe and His Blue Grass Boys on a summer evening in 1946, when I was six years old. Boy, this really *tattooed my brain.* I've never forgotten it: Bill had a real good five-piece band. They took that old hillbilly music, sped it up, and basically invented what is now known as blue-grass music: the bass, in its place, the mandolin above it, the guitar tying the two together, and the violin on top, playing the long notes to make it sing. The banjo backed the whole thing up, answering everybody. We heard Bill Monroe regularly on the *Grand Ole Opry,* but here he was in the flesh. Lester Flatt and Earl Scruggs were in the band when I saw them.

That was the end of cowboys and Indians for me. When I got home I held the broom sideward and strutted past the barn, around the pump, and out to the watermelon patch, pretending to play the guitar. I was hooked.

. . . Whenever one of the big traveling shows came to town, the Helms would be there. Silas Green from New Orleans had a twelve-piece orchestra that we all liked, but everyone's favorite was the F. S. Walcott Rabbits Foot Minstrels from, I believe, Biloxi, Mississippi. Posters and handbills would go up weeks in advance. They'd set up with the back of a big truck as the stage, a fast-talking master of ceremonies, a good-looking mulatto chorus line, blackface comedians and singers. This was like another world for us kids.

. . . Our favorite act was "The Lady with the Million Dollar Smile," F. S. Walcott's big featured singer, who'd come on in the third quarter of the show. She was an *armful*. She wore very bright dresses and had all her teeth filled with diamonds! She sang all those real get-down songs like "Shake a Hand." Later on the master of ceremonies would announce, "Ladies and Gentlemen, it's been a great evening. We haven't played a show this good since New Orleans! I sure wish every night could be this good. Now it's time for what we call the Midnight Ramble. I know a lot of you have to get up early and get to work, and a lot of you have your families with you, and we want to thank all of you for coming and wish you well till next year. In the meantime, for those of you who can stay late and have a mind for more sophisticated entertainment . . . " He'd introduce one of the beautiful dancers from the four-girl chorus line and tell us how Caledonia would show us what made her famous down in Miami, Florida, where she hails from.

The Midnight Ramble cost another dollar, dollar and a half. You'd see what in those days was defined as a hootchy-kootchy show. The comedians would do some of their raunchier material, and people'd be holding their sides. The band would get into its louder rumba-style things, and the dancers would come out in outfits that would be right in style today but were bare and outrageous back then. The master of ceremonies might get caught up in it and jig across the stage like a chicken or anything familiar from the barnyard, which always set the crowd off. That was the Midnight Ramble, so called because it usually ended at twelve o'clock.

Today, when folks ask me where rock and roll came from, I always think of our southern medicine shows and that wild Midnight Ramble. Chuck Berry's duck walk, Elvis Presley's rockabilly gyrations, Little Richard's dancing on the piano, Jerry Lee Lewis's antics, and Ronnie Hawkin's camel walk could have come right off F. S. Walcott's stage. (13–22)

Jeannie Whayne

I was born in 1948 so I grew up in the early sixties . I guess one of the things that was unique about my family was this: my father was a pharmacist but he was also a gambler, and he raised greyhound dogs. So we would go to the dog track in West Memphis, and my mother and father would go into the dog track and leave us in the parking lot. And there was this whole culture of kids who hung around in the parking lot at the dog track while their parents went to the races. And it was just wild. It was great fun; we didn't think there was anything wrong with it, didn't feel in any danger. We were completely at our own discretion. It was an amazing experience as I look back on it. Today you wouldn't think of leaving your children like that, but it was, I guess, a different time. You weren't worried about a psychopath picking up your children. Sometimes I would babysit for people who had a small child. I was small myself, relatively ten or eleven, and I remember one time this woman left me with her little kid, and when she got back, her car was covered with popcorn because I had no ability to control this child.

My brother and sister and I got to know the signs when my mother and father came back to the car, whether he had done well or not. If he had done well, we stopped for dinner, had a steak or something somewhere at one o'clock in the morning. If he hadn't, silence in the car all the way home. At some point, maybe when I was about eleven or twelve, the greyhound track got nervous about it and wouldn't let people leave kids in their cars anymore. At that point my parents would drop us off at the movie theater. I don't think they were scrupulous then about watching who was getting in to see some of those movies because I'm sure I saw some I shouldn't have been seeing. I remember being utterly confused. I remember my mother gave me a little book on the facts of life that I don't think I read because I remember not being able to understand what was going on on the movie screen. We enjoyed that, and sometimes my mother and father wouldn't get there before they closed the movie theater, and we'd stand out on the sidewalk and wait sometimes a half an hour or an hour. This was at night, in West Memphis, Arkansas, not in the best part of town, but we weren't scared. That's probably why we didn't do very well in school for a long time.

Shirley Abbott

The most vivid memories of my childhood are long afternoons when my aunt Vera would come to our house with her daughter, June, and the four of us would form a kind of subversive cell. June and I would usually play, indoors and out, while our mothers sewed or quilted or canned. Sometimes the four of us would dress and get in the car and drive around Hot Springs, buying thread and snaps at the dry-goods store, visiting some spring or other and drinking from tin cups, or "ratting up and down," as my aunt called it, on Central Avenue. Hearing what they said on these afternoons, I gradually realized that my mother and her sister were not awed by men in the least, that they preferred each other's company to that of their respective husbands.

. . . Often I spent summer afternoons in larger groups of women, not my kin. The neighborhood beauty shop is one of the foundations of society in small southern towns. You go there to get your hair fixed, but that isn't the real reason, any more than men congregate at the county courthouse to transact legal business. The beauty operator is invariably a middle-aged woman who found herself in need of a trade and solved the problem by getting her license and having some shampoo sinks and hair dryers installed on the glassed-in porch. All the neighborhood women would have standing appointments, as my mother did, and they'd bring their children along. It was an all female society—no man would dare enter the place—and here, if nowhere else, women said what they thought about men. And what they thought was often fairly murderous. . . . The leitmotif of the song they sang was their loyalty and fortitude in the face of male foolishness, and as a keen obbligato, "Don't ever let them know what you really think of them. Humor them. Pretend you love them. Even love them, if you must. But play a strong card to their weak one." . . . This was their means to survival, a minority strategy worked out and handed along from mother to daughter. (167–69)

Grif Stockley

Sunday afternoons were my time with Daddy. . . . They were very devout Presbyterians, so we always had to go to Sunday school and church. It was absolutely boring and Daddy would always go to sleep, and I would sit beside him and be the one to nudge him awake. And he would give me the sweetest smile when I would wake him up as though he hadn't meant to fall asleep.

We'd go home from church and have typical Sunday dinner: fabulous foods like fried chicken and mashed potatoes, turnip greens, rolls, and iced tea. I've still never found anybody who could cook turnip greens and strawberry shortcake like Mother did.

We had beagles and Daddy and I went hunting, but it was mainly just an excuse to get outside. We hardly ever killed anything, but one of the things Daddy and I did, we would go out in the truck to the St. Francis bridge, and we would shoot. And this seems horrible to me now, but one of the things we did was take a .22 rifle and shoot gar and turtles off that bridge. It just seems cruel as it could be. . . .

I remember one time Daddy and I went out on the trestle over the river, and we heard a train coming and had to run back. And Daddy kept saying, "Grif, you've got to go faster." Otherwise, we would have had to jump off the trestle. It was pretty scary. But we made it back and told that story, and Mother was horrified, but it was always a story we liked to tell.

Another thing I remember, in the summer I would come down the stairs, and Daddy would be gone to work by seven. And I would come down and sit in his spot, and Mother would have laid out the sports pages in the [Memphis] Commercial Appeal for me. And I'd sit there kind of like I was a little prince; the king had gone off to work, and here was the son, the heir apparent. I always had the same breakfast, and I would sit there and read the sports pages. And then I would go outside, and sometimes there would be two African American men, Andrew and Duke, doing the flower beds. And I would call them by their first names and they would call me Mr. Grif, and I would take food out to them at noon, and they would sit in the garage and eat dinner and drink out of the hydrant. I don't know where they went to the bathroom. I was the kind of kid who watched the news—and it wasn't like I didn't know that the civil rights movement had started—but we existed in a cocoon over there and would not allow ourselves to realize.

Delta Willis

b. 1948, Watson, Desha County. Writer, Senior communications director of the National Audubon Society. From an unpublished essay, 2010.

One night after supper I went frog gigging with my father and his men friends. I don't remember the friends but I remember that everyone had a headlamp but me. Slowly paddling about in an aluminum Johnboat they plucked huge bullfrogs from the water's edge with a gig, a metal-mouth trap on the end of a long wooden pole. (It's the kind of contraption I long for in Manhattan when I see so many plastic bags hung in the trees, carried there by street canyon thermals and subway draft.)

The Cottonmouth Moccasin is a venomous pit viper found in the slow-moving bayous that cut through the delta. When competitive or threatened, it will gape, exposing the white lining of its mouth. That night, as the lights cast around the boat, full of us and bloody, dying frogs, Cottonmouths swayed in the black night air, their heads high out of the water. Of course, the men's beams were looking for more frogs to gig so there were long sweeps away from my focus when I wondered where these snakes had gone in the dark, whether they had succeeded in getting into the boat.

This image did more than strike me, it stuck with me. During my twenties and thirties, I awoke from nightmares where I couldn't speak, couldn't say what needed to be said. I woke gaping, yet felt my mouth had been stuffed with cotton.

I'm not sure of how old I was on this midnight ramble, perhaps as young as five, certainly under eight, long before the insecurities of puberty but small enough to ride on my father's neck, which is how I recall reaching the boat and leaving it, unscathed. Of course, I longed to direct his headlamp but there was this fantastic, sentimental trust for his skills as a pilot in the dark which endured for half a century. He knew where he was going and I followed him in the dark on night hunts like this, spotlighting deer, camping out beneath canvas, my young mind enjoying glimpses of extraordinary things and spaces of dark where my imagination went wild. These outdoor adventures established the plot for the rest of my life, whether driving 4-wheel drive vehicles across the Sahara, tracking lions by night or observing gala theater openings in New York City where spotlights crisscross the night sky, knowing that above whatever is in the dark, there is a canopy of stars.

Killing never appealed to me but I went hunting to be in the woods, to savor stories told around a campfire, to walk in the footsteps of bear and to sense the great, complicated quiet of the wilderness. We often sat for hours, not speaking, just listening. Beavers might work away noisily nearby, and on the river there were great surprising sounds like a bank calving or trees crashing. We sometimes slept on houseboats or rustic hideaways that served as hunting clubs. Largely the exclusive retreat of men, some clubs were cabins with bunk beds; none had curtains or indoor toilets, but for a girl who resembled a tap-dancing Shirley Temple, these male retreats held a delicious sense of being in *verboten* terrain. That the camp cook was on loan from the local prison or that every man in the camp was running away from something would prepare me for mean streets in New York and Nairobi and the guile of sweet talkers.

Getting to these woods was an adventure we undertook in a Ford Model A outfitted with a flatbed for carrying a boat. Behind the only two front seats was a toolbox where I sometimes slept on top of a blanket. We learned to read spoor, to be quiet in order to hear nature and to step lively when the log we stepped on turned out to be a rattlesnake. They could be thicker than the great old tree vines, and their length stretched along the car's running boards from front wheel to back.

LaVerne Feaster

If we didn't go to church, we couldn't go out on Sunday. If I stayed home, I couldn't go out that day. On Sunday we would get up and go to our Sunday school and church, and then we would go back home and eat dinner. And then at three o'clock we'd go to the movies. All the black people sat upstairs, and we could see the man back there shooting the show, and the noise was back there where he was but we were all up there on the balcony. And then when the movie was over, we would go to our youth activities at each church, to the Presbyterian for Youth Endeavour, and the League at the Methodist church, and at the Baptist church there were activities. And then when it was over, we would all meet at the Sanctified church and watch them testify and dance, and then we'd all go home. We'd get in trouble if we made fun of them. They were in a little booth, and if we didn't respect them, we'd get in some bad trouble. But we'd go there and try to hold our laughs back while they'd be shouting and carrying on. There'd be adults there also watching them, from the various churches that were not sanctified either, that would watch them testify and dance and sing. It was kind of an activity, like a movie.

Sometimes we would go to activities at other churches. The Baptists and Presbyterian kids might go to the Methodists on this Sunday, and all of us would go to the Baptist church next Sunday, and then to the Presbyterian the Sunday after that. Everybody loved to come to the Presbyterian church because they could go up in the pulpit and stand behind it. And there the youths could all take sacrament, and in the Baptist church they couldn't. And we didn't disrespect them or think they weren't as good as we were, we just felt that those were their rules. We would have Easter at one church and Christmas at another church, and we'd have our speeches and groups would sing and whatever. That was our Sunday routine.

There were rules. We couldn't get up and go out of the church. We couldn't get up and go to the bathroom except between Sunday school and church. We couldn't even look back when the door opened.

And sometimes after church we'd have dinner there. Had no refrigeration; Mama and them would have to go home and get the cold pops and ice, but that food, chicken and all that other food, would be sitting out there in those wagons under the trees 'til we got through with church. And nobody would get sick! Now if you cook something and don't put it in the refrigerator the next minute, it will spoil.

Randall C. Ferguson Jr.

I always had a desire to do well at whatever I did, and I really tried to do that. I also had a strong desire to want to please my parents and I knew that working hard, making good grades, all those things, would please them. And I did not want to disappoint them, I mean I was just driven to just be the best that I could be. . . . I was around people who worked hard. I mean, we weren't allowed, for instance, to get up and leave our room without having made our bed. You don't even walk out the door. I mean, you don't even walk in the kitchen. I mean, you made your bed when you got up. . . . That's just the way it was in my house. You clean up behind yourself. We all learned to wash dishes at an early age. . . . The expectation was there: "You ought to work hard. You can be anything you want to be if you just don't give up. And guess what! You're going to have to work awfully hard. And every Sunday I was hearing it in church all the time. You even heard it in kindergarten. . . . I remember coming home with a report card that had seventeen A's and three B's on it. This was in elementary school. . . . I showed it to my mother. She just [said], "Oh, I'm so proud of you," and showed it to my father. He looked at it and said, "Where did these B's come from?" (38–39)

Karen Rudolph Shoffner

Church was a huge deal, a big part of our social lives You had to have an affiliation. Ours was St. Paul's Episcopal Church. We went to church on Sunday, then Sunday school after that. Each of us got involved with Episcopal Young Churchmen in junior high which gave us the opportunity to go to places like Little Rock for events and gatherings of different kinds. We went to the Episcopal church's Camp Mitchell on Mount Petit Jean in the summer.

I can't carry a tune but I sang in the choir. Every Saturday I had to go to choir practice, but Saturday morning was also the only time we got to watch television. My favorite shows came on at ten and ten thirty, so it was a question of how fast you could walk to get there before Mrs. Lindloff, the choir director, screamed at you for being late. There were big issues. One was that to get to the church you had to cross Dickson Street alone. There was lots of freedom, but there were big streets you couldn't cross. Dickson was one of them.

Mary Elsie Robertson

b. 1937, near Charleston, Franklin County. Writer.
Interview with Margaret Bolsterli, 2010.

My family was Baptist, First Baptist Church in Charleston. Daddy was a deacon for fifty years or something. Both my parents taught Sunday school classes. They were very much involved, so of course I was taken to church from the time I was a baby. When I was five, I suddenly actually heard what the preacher was saying. Up to that point, it had just been clouds over my head. I hadn't really paid any attention, but when

I actually heard, what I heard was," If you die and you're not saved, you're going to go to hell." And that set off a really hideous part of my childhood. Because, for reasons I don't fully understand, I did not, I could not say anything to anybody about this. But I was tormented. I thought, and it's a reasonable assumption if you've gone to Baptist sermons for even five years that what you needed to do was walk down to the front of the church and that was pretty much it. But I guess the assumption was that if you walk down to the front of the church you are saying either, "I want to be saved," or "I believe in Jesus," or something. But I could not make myself do that. I could not do it. I made myself sick. Every summer, I would be sick; I couldn't eat. Mother took me to doctors, and I was given vitamins and cod liver oil. I was just scared; I was scared to death. It did not occur to anybody in my family, although they were loving, and generally speaking, pretty understanding people, and I couldn't say anything.

So this went on. When I was eleven, I finally did, at vacation Bible school, and because friends of mine were going down the aisle, I went down the aisle too and then was sitting kind of miserably on the front pew and the preacher came around saying, "Do you believe that Jesus is the son of God. And I said, "Well of course." I'd heard it all my life; what other possibility was there? But this changed nothing. I felt nothing. You're supposed to feel this elation, this peace. I didn't feel anything. And that made things worse, in a way. You've done what you were supposed to do and it didn't work. I continued suffering over it.

Then, when I was in the sixth grade, two things happened. One was that I had, that year, for the first time several different teachers, and I had Betty Flanagan, before she married Dale Bumpers, as my English and art teacher. She had gone away. She had lived in Chicago. She had lived a somewhat unusual life for Charleston, and I was highly taken with her. I had a crush on her, there's no question. I think that that kind of lifted me in a way out of that little tiny, enclosed world that I couldn't seem to get out of. Also, and this is going to sound kind of crazy, but I haunted the town library. I read everything, and there came a time when I had read all of the children and teenager books. I'd read all of them, and usually more than once.

And I needed new books. So one day I went sort of uncertainly over to the adult section and was just walking up and down looking for something and what I came up with was *The Brothers Karamazov*. Weird title, weird writer's name. I really thought that when I took it up to the librarian, who knew me very well, that she might not let me have an adult book. But she just looked at *Dostoevsky* and said, "I wonder how you pronounce that." Of course I had no idea.

Of course it was way over my head in all kinds of ways, but it was concerned with religion, with god, with the nature of god, and I had had a lifetime of those questions. So it spoke, as Quakers say, "to my condition." Much of it was totally over my head. I couldn't make much sense out of some of it, but some of it I could, and that opened the door. And I realized that this god thing is not exactly what I had been led to believe. There was something much more there. And following those two things, and I distinctly remember when it happened: I was feeding the chickens, throwing the chops out, and I thought, "You know what, you've been in hell all along. And I'm sick of it." I just say, "No." And that ended it. From then on I just couldn't concern myself with the hell question. I concerned myself with the god question but very differently. And it's very important to me. I've become a Quaker; I suspect because it is the only form of organized religion that is as little organized as it is possible to be.

Holly Boone

b. 1954, Fort Smith, Sebastian County. Writer.
From a memory written for this collection, April 2010.

This is how I got saved. It was a blistering Sunday evening in 1962. I was eight, my sister ten. We had been sent to our maternal grandparents for the summer while our parents tried to patch things up one more time at home in Fort Smith. Staying with Granny always meant a lot of church. Every Sunday morning and Sunday evening, too, if there was a singing or, as that night, a revival. The guest evangelist, a stocky, balding man who looked too old for me to call *brother*, seemed prepared to speak all night. Granny did not allow my sister and me to write notes to each other on the bulletin or flip through the blue hymnal looking for funny words. My boredom was almost a physical ache.

As Baptist ministers tended to do in those days, Brother eventually came around to the subject of hell. The cadenced boom and swell of his voice dropped to a slow whisper. "Have you ever smelled burning human flesh?" At last he had my attention. "Well, Brothers and Sisters"—dramatic pause—"I have." He was witness to a hotel fire in "a large Eastern city." He described in some detail the screams of the dying and the "nauseating" aroma of burning human beings. "Do you want to burn, too? Do you want your loved ones to burn in everlasting fire?"

Suddenly I was intensely lonely for my parents, afraid for them. What if Mother and Daddy were this minute burning up in a hotel? What if they were burning up in our house in Fort Smith? Mother was always leaving a cigarette to smolder on the edge of our char-speckled kitchen table or her bedside stand.

By then everyone was singing "Softly and Tenderly Jesus is Calling," a hymn deliberately crafted to spring souls straight from the pew. I imagined my mother's face at a blazing, high-storied window, calling for help, calling for me. I began to cry. Always my sympathizer, my sister began to cry too. Pleased with this development, Granny nudged us out into the aisle. Then my sister and I were standing down front with a few other sobbing candidates for salvation, our faces slick with tears. Brother took our hands and leaned his bushy eyebrows close and asked if we accepted Jesus Christ as our personal savior. Feeling every eye on us and especially Granny's, we nodded our sniveling heads. A few Sundays later, no further questions asked on either side, we got dunked in the tank behind the altar.

This memory, which still illuminates for me a strain of irresponsible theology, unexamined belief, and brainless emotionalism common to religious expression in the South, is one reason I no longer live there. That and chiggers.

Julie Gabel

b. 1958, Fayetteville, Washington County. IT administrator.
Interview with Margaret Bolsterli, 2010.

I grew up in Fayetteville, on Hall Avenue, and we knew all our neighbors. My brothers and sisters were all older than I and were gone while I was still a child and my parents were married for fifty-four years. . . . I felt very secure and taken care of and confident. And most of my friends were similar. . . . Back then it was mostly both parents in the home. And my siblings and I are all married to the first person we started with, which is rare.

Michael Thomas

b. 1963, Farmington, Washington County. Teacher, actor, writer.
Interview with Margaret Bolsterli, 2010.

Farmington then, in 1963, was just the outskirts of Fayetteville. My mom worked in Fayetteville, and I went to school in Fayetteville. Brookside was a brand new addition on the Fayetteville side of Farmington, and we were the first house on the right in that addition.

The strongest memory that comes right to mind was my father's death when I was five years old. That kind of shadowed everything else. It was a big moment. That is, it was the man I thought was my father—it came out thirty years later that he wasn't, but the man who I assumed then was my father. His name was Hulen, and he opened the farmers' coop in Fayetteville. He was a seed salesman, had a college degree. I really looked up to him, and the stories I heard later about him wanting to be like Humphrey Bogart, wearing his hat that way, made me admire him even more. It seems like it was the wintertime, December or January that morning in 1968. And it was my job on Saturday mornings to wake him up because we had a big breakfast then. He was diabetic and had lost both his legs by that time. . . . So I went in to wake him up that morning and something was wrong.

He was cold; he didn't feel right to me. The covers weren't on him. The smell of bacon was in the air, and that usually got him up. I went and told Mom, "He's not getting up. He's not getting up" and went back to my coloring book, and she went in. And from then on, it was very strange. I could tell there was something wrong because there was both crying and smiling. She was trying to control herself in front of me. That was a big, traumatic time. He was wheeled out of the house on a stretcher. He'd had a heart attack in the night. And everybody started coming in the house. He had been in the hospital quite a few times. He would go in and come back, go in and come back. . . . So I thought, as a five-year-old, he was just going to the hospital again. There was something about heaven in the air though. People were talking about how "he'll be walking now. He'll be walking the streets of heaven now with his legs." And as a kid I thought, "Oh, good, he'll be getting those legs he wanted and coming back." It was just a bunch of mixed messages I was getting from people. Everybody meant well, but the stories were confusing to a child.

Later, my great-aunt Carlene was the one that told me. She got real jealous there at the end because my mom was getting all the attention from the family because of her Alzheimer's. And Carlene was old, but she didn't have Alzheimer's, and she wanted some attention. And she didn't like all the attention Joyce, my mom, was getting. I was helping her out of the car. . . . I was about thirty . . . and she said, "You know, Hulen wasn't your father. She never told you, but Hulen wasn't your father. Your mom cheated on him. She had an affair and Hulen just took you in."

I grew up there in Brookside until I was nine. . . . My mom started dating about a year later, after Hulen died, and I went though two or three dads there. She married two men while we lived there, and the third man, Norman, stayed with us the longest. He became *Dad*. He was a truck driver. Norman leaves and comes back into my life several times. My mom was married, I think, six times in all from the time I was five until I was sixteen. She actually went through a marriage and everything. Like Elizabeth Taylor, she was. My idea of fathers, growing up, were TV dads, those good American wholesome dads:

Leave it to Beaver's dad. Those were those fifties good, American wholesome dads. I thought, "That's what a dad's supposed to be like: Marcus Welby and Andy Griffith and Ward Cleaver. Ah, that's what a dad's supposed to be like." Because I never really had a dad, growing up. Even my friends' dads, I couldn't quite tell even from them what a dad was supposed to be like. It's interesting that some of the fathers I had don't stand out as much as some of the friends.

. . . Norman was a great big man, a truck driver. He looked like John Wayne to me. A great big guy from Louisiana, a self-proclaimed *coon-ass*. A big, scary man until you got to know him, and then you saw he was a big softy. He was loving to us. He was gone on the truck a lot, though. That seemed to suit Mom's style: she could be on her own and have the house to herself and then have a husband when he was home.

. . . We ate together and that was important. We sat down at the table. Norm was a big cook and Mom liked to cook, so we had sit-down dinners. And I always blame my later weight on that. Norman was a big rice eater. We had rice at every meal, rice and gravy with pork chops or steaks or chicken, always a heavy meal. And Mom would fix two or three vegetable-type things, and you had to eat all that was on your plate. They fixed my plate; I didn't pick my food. My plate was made for me, and I had to eat it. You don't waste food. It was a big, big deal not to waste food. I remember many nights sitting there alone with the clock ticking, the table's cleaned, the kitchen's empty, and I just can't eat any more. So I learned that you don't leave anything on the plate, no matter where you are.

Norman was really big on "yes ma'am" and "no ma'am," and I tried. . . . And there were no elbows on the table, and you did not chew with your mouth open. And then when he was on the truck and gone for two weeks at a time, we would still try to have those dinners, but it was not quite the same. We had a family member who worked for Swanson's, so he was always dropping off TV dinners for us. And then the TV trays came out, and we ate watching TV.

When we moved into Fayetteville, we moved into the Villa Mobile Home Trailer Park. And I really liked that trailer. It was a double-wide and a neat place to live. But the kids in the trailer park were different from the kids in my Brookside neighborhood; I couldn't make friends there. I was in fights. They were tough kids who hung out in the laundry room and played quarters, throwing quarters against the wall. And there were older kids there, not kids my age. Those years from about age nine I spent a lot of time watching TV. We lived there three or four years.

We would visit my sister in Fort Smith, and I played with a lot of kids there. . . . My cousin Grant lived down there, and I credit him with getting me started in the theater. We used to tell stories. We'd sit around and tell stories and make up stuff. It was a mixture of family and cartoons, and we would tell stories, and I could always crack him up. I can remember the exact time and place when he said, "You ought to be an actor, you are so funny, you ought to be an actor!"

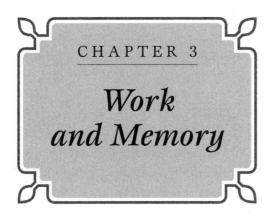

CHAPTER 3

Work and Memory

Most children were expected to take responsibilities around the house and yard for the common good of the family. From an early age they washed dishes and clothes, milked cows, fed chickens, gathered eggs, pumped water, drew water from wells, and even cleaned out wells; in short, they did whatever needed to be done. Chores, for most children, were simply part of the territory of family life that fell to their lot.

Depending on the family's circumstances, other work was frequently added to the burden of chores. Before the mechanization of farming, children, sometimes starting at the age of five, provided much of the labor needed in the fields. In cotton fields, this work included stoop labor at its most brutal. People remember vividly the hard work and sweltering days, but it is significant that every one of these memories includes some redeeming factor about that work and those times. Most say that while they would not want their children to have to work that hard, they do not regret having done it—having survived it themselves. They treasure the lessons learned and the memory of the pleasures of camaraderie. Families drew closer through the shared experience, and the cotton fields seem to have provided a respite from overt racism. Out there, under that hot sun, black and white were all in it together.

Adolescents also worked in sawmills, canning factories, grocery stores, and delivery trucks. Frequently boys as young as twelve were the drivers who drove the truck or wagon hauling cotton to the gin at night and were expected to be back in the field again early in the morning.

In the early part of our time period, in somewhat better-off families, the work of choice for girls as young as fifteen was teaching in a one-room school. The qualification for this was a license acquired by passing a county examination. Still children themselves, they often had the daunting task of keeping order among pupils older than they, which they were able to do because they had the support of the parents to an extent rarely seen in later times.

Pearl Lou Mattmiller Katz

We had a work ethic for the whole family. Time never hung on our hands. There was always something to do. We had a smokehouse about twenty steps away from the house and near this smoke house every fall our father killed, with the help of neighbors, about eight hogs. And he cut them up into hams and middlings and shoulders and salted them down, and when they had taken the salt, he washed the salt off the outside of them and hung them up from the rafters in the smokehouse. And it was the children's job, after a fire was lit under them, to keep up the smoke. We had hickory chips—corncobs to start the fire and then hickory chips to keep the smoke going for days and days until that meat was saturated with the smoke, which gave it that delicious flavor when it was eaten. In this smokehouse we also had a barrel in which we kept our sorghum. Every year we planted sorghum cane, and we children would rip the cane and cut it down and lay it across the rows. And the wagon would come along and pick it up and take it to the sorghum mill. Our barrel held between fifty and sixty gallons of molasses. And we found that very, very good with biscuits in the mornings with ham or sausage. But in addition to that, in the smokehouse we put up the peaches and apples and pears we didn't eat fresh.

Also in the back of the house we had a milk house. And at first we used to keep a trough that ran through the milk house from the well on its way to another trough where the horses drank water. We would draw a bucket of water and pour it in this trough, and it would run through and cool the milk and then go on out and do its second job feeding the horses water. Later on we got a separator and did not need the troughs anymore. The cream would go to the creamery in Gillett, and the milk would be fed to the calves. We didn't have a special place for the cows to be milked. We let them into the lot and let the calves go to them, and then we put a loop around the calves' noses and pulled them off and tied them and milked the cows. Then afterwards we turned the calves loose, and they could go to their mothers again. But we had gotten most of the milk by that time, and we fed the separated milk to the calves. Later on, of course, people have made a big job out of raising milk. But this was just a by-product with us. We drank plenty of the milk ourselves.

. . . We had the barn and a hay mow, and we had a lot of hay because the prairie back of us was open and anyone could get hay and take it home whenever they wanted to. So we had hay in the barn and stacks of hay put up around a pole behind the barn. The chickens often made their nests in this hay that was in the barn, and it was a lot of fun to find a nest with quite a number of eggs in it.

Close to it and closer to the highway was our cotton pen and corncrib. We would go down there and get our own corn and shuck it and take it to our Uncle Fred's mill. One time there was a snake in there when we were getting some corn. And it would watch us and we would watch it, and we knew that it was a king snake and would not hurt us but we kept our eye on it. . . . . I was not afraid of snakes because many times I have picked blackberries on vines fastened to a thorn tree on the limb of which a snake was lying out full length, but I was never afraid of that because I thought that it would have to be coiled to strike. We canned berries, and whatever we didn't need we took to Gillett in gallon jars and sold.

When we worked in the fields, we got very brown but we wanted to look white and tender like a city girl would look, and we heard that buttermilk took the color out of things. We figured that if you could take the mildew out of a piece of cloth by putting it in buttermilk, you could take the freckles and tan off of us with it. So we conceived the idea of rubbing it on our faces and necks and arms and hands. It smelled bad and Mammy would not allow us to sleep in the bed and get the buttermilk on the bedclothes, so we had to sleep in the wagon bed out in the yard. We took a bowl of buttermilk with us, and from time to time we'd put another layer of buttermilk on. So I guess we smelled to high heaven by the time we came in the next morning when we had to wash it off. But we did that several nights. The mosquitoes got pretty bad, and I remember one night when we went up in the barn loft and slept on the cotton seeds and applied the buttermilk. But it never did us much good.

There were eight girls of us in the family, and we did practically everything that a farm needs to have done except plow and split wood. We didn't do that. Our daddy did not want us to risk doing something with an ax and hurting ourselves. And he felt sure we couldn't hold a plow as it went down a row of cotton or corn. But we did everything else under the sun. I want to say that I am not sorry for any of the work I did. I picked cotton, I picked peas, I picked berries, I hoed cotton and thinned corn, and all that sort of thing, and I was glad I could do it and could still do some of it now. And I am eighty-nine years old!

Bonnie Brashears Pace

**b. 1905, Combs, Madison County. Retired teacher.
Interview with Margaret Bolsterli, 1997.**

I got my teaching certificate by taking the county examination when I was fifteen years old. My first school was at Fairview near the junction of Highway 23 and Highway 16. One of my uncles was on the school board, so I had to go to every home that had children in the home and get a petition signed because if you had a relative on the school board you had to. I rode a horse to all the families in that district. Of course at that time, you didn't cut your hair or wear pants, and my mother had a side saddle and skirt that went with it. I was fifteen years old, and I went to those places riding that horse.

I got the school, and my uncle told me to be real tough at the beginning, so I had to whip seven the first day. I had some boys seventeen, and I was only fifteen but they didn't know it. I weighed a little more and was a couple of inches taller then than I am now, and I had worked with my brothers on the farm and I was strong. What they did, we had no glass in the windows, and when I turned them loose for recess, some of them jumped out the windows. We had long benches for them to sit on. They had about a fifteen minute recess around ten o'clock, and when they came back in, I talked to them. I said, "We don't do it that way. Where I went to school we went out the door, and you must do that too. I don't want anybody to do this again. This will get you in trouble. You have to get out of your seats, line up, and walk out the door." I had a little bell to shake to bring the children in. When I turned them loose for lunch, they did the same thing again. At least seven of them did. So I told them my punishment was a spanking if they didn't mind me, and when they went out for lunch, I went out and cut a hickory limb. That's what they used in those days. We had a long bench in front where they all sat to recite, and I just called them up to the recitation bench and I whipped them. And that ended that, and I didn't whip any more the rest of the term except two boys that got in a fight and had brought knives to school. They were not allowed to bring knives to school. One was my age, but he didn't know it. The other was seventeen. The older one said he wasn't going to take a whipping; he was so big and all. The fifteen-year-old said, "Yeah, I'll take mine and stay here." I said to the other one, "You'll have to go home if you don't take your whipping." So he left for a little while and came back and said, "You'd just as well to whip me because my folks will bring me back." And they would have at that time because they were behind me on this. So I whipped him.

It was just a three-months school. I made lesson plans. I worked with the first graders and taught them phonics and things. I had a girl that was seventeen and two or three others close to my age, and I would take some of these to help those little fellows when I had assigned a lesson. I would say "Help this one," while I had the next class. We didn't have any kindergarten, so in the first grade we were getting them sometimes at five years old. So I'd have somebody take the second-grade lesson, and I would hear these first and second graders at least two times a day. The little ones listened to the big ones. And you combined the third and fourth grades to spell together. And you could have the first and second spell some of those little words they were just learning.

Beatrice Sharp Bell

b. 1912, Wesley, Madison County. Self-described "Retired Jack of All Trades." Interview with Margaret Bolsterli, 1997.

I worked in the fields. I chopped corn, and that was awful. A lot of Johnson grass down there looked just like corn. You couldn't tell the Johnson grass from the corn. I had to be the boss, more or less. My brothers wanted to go to Richland Creek and look for fish. We had a time down there. I was the straw boss, just two years older than my older brother!

We ate quite a bit of chicken. I have dressed chickens ever since I was big enough to build a fire outside and heat water in an old black teakettle to scald them. Then we would have chicken for breakfast and take it to school for lunch.

We had a canning factory here, and I would stand on a crate because I wasn't tall enough to reach the bucket. And I think that first year I made twenty-some-odd dollars, and I thought I was rich. I suppose I was thirteen or fourteen or something like that. And all the other kids did the same thing. And, actually, that was the first time that the women around here had had a chance to make a little money. It felt good; it really did. At that time we bought our own basketballs at school, and we tried awful hard to get fifty cents together to contribute what we were supposed to. And I always saved my fifty cents for that.

Zeraldine Daniel Gladden

b. 1917, Yell County, moved to rural Desha County, near Watson, in 1928. Interview with Margaret Bolsterli, 1986.

Oh in Yell County we had good water, deep wells and good water. I remember we lived in a nice big house before we moved down here [Desha County]. The well was on the back porch, and lots of times our water'd get to smelling bad. And of course we had to do something about it. I was the one. I was just eleven when we moved down here, but I did this for I don't know how many years before we moved. I can remember my dad and older brother drawing that well dry just bucket after bucket 'til they got it almost dry. Then they'd tie a stick of stove wood on the well rope, and I would get on that stick of stove wood and they'd let me down in that well. There might be a dead rabbit in it, maybe a chicken had fallen in, or something else was dropped in there, and they wanted it out. I went down and cleaned it out or did whatever was to be done.

After my brothers left home I was Dad's boy. I took the team and plowed all day, worked in the hay, things like that. I was healthy and strong, and I wanted to do it. I thought that was bigger than chopping cotton or something like that. I felt very important. My dad bought eighty acres of land up at Repo, and I would get in the wagon of a morning early, carry my lunch, and go to Repo and plow all day. And then come in about dark. I felt very important, of course.

After school was started we were just in the height of picking cotton, so we had to keep picking. And maybe we'd start school two weeks late. And then maybe later on, Dad might have something he needed to do, and he'd keep us all out a day to pick. And the same way, we stayed out in spring to chop cotton if he felt it necessary. And naturally we were critical of him then, and it made us mad and all, but he wouldn't have done it if he hadn't needed it so bad.

William H. Bowen

My first venture into the world of work outside the home—where we cut kindling, mowed the yard, raked the leaves, and milked the cow—was carrying water and sharpening axes and hoes on a ditch-clearing effort on our farm in the summer of 1934. The work allowed me to save enough money for two weeks of scout camp at Camp Caudle in Russellville. I went with my cousin, John Rankin, that summer. Our camp adjoined the Illinois Bayou, where the water was amazingly clear compared to the murky waters of our Flat Bayou. I was greatly impressed. Camp Caudle was unique in that one of our challenges was to build our own cabin accommodations. But what can you expect for $2.50 per week?

My father, together with two partners, Louis Altheimer and Willis Clary, founded the ABC Store . . . and he also shared ownership of the Altheimer Cotton Gin. As a child, I worked in the store and cotton gin at various times. In the store, I stocked shelves, served customers, and was also assistant butcher. The store had two front doors. The one on the east side of the building opened into the "dry goods" department where we stocked women's dresses, overalls, and other items. On the west side were the groceries. In another room, we sold feed, seed, and fertilizer. When I worked as a butcher, we sold mostly pig feet and neck bones with the meat pretty much taken off. We also had round steak and it was always the same. It was never broiled because it was not a good enough cut. It was cooked with a sort of gravy and quite often we added tomatoes and okra. I loved it. I distinctly remember in the navy when I first ate a grilled steak, I did not think they had cooked it properly.

I also ran the gristmill at the gin on Saturdays in the fall. There we ground whole grain into cornmeal. My day began early—my first duty of the day was to make sure there was enough kindling for my father to start a fire in the living room stove. I learned early on to make sure I cut the kindling the night before because, if not, my body was roused and I would go out in the dark and cut kindling. My tasks also included going to the ABC Store every Thursday to get twenty dollars in cash. We used the money for household expenses and paid the cook and laundress each a dollar a week.

When I was thirteen, I tried my hand at farming, taking charge of a thirteen-acre cotton crop on what we called Tupelo Break. My father wanted at least one of his sons to farm. My older brother, Bob, worked in the cotton gin and my brother John called himself an "oil horizontal transfer engineer"—big words for working in a filling station and pumping gas into cars. Heavy rains destroyed most of my crop that year and I decided at an early age that whatever I did with my life, it would not be farming if I could help it. By the time the water had subsided the plot was pretty barren and there was a stalk alive about every ten feet. That ended my farming career. (7–11)

Raymond Riggins

Even as a little boy out there on Cypress Creek, I had jobs. I found out that you could sell *Grit* newspapers. And I don't know how many customers I had, but every week they would send me a bundle of *Grit* newspapers, and I had my route. I sold those papers, and I sold Rosebud salve that was an all-purpose salve that I guess would cure cancer. It was supposed to cure anything you might have wrong with you. I found out I could sell products on their merits, not necessarily because I was a cute little boy. Back there in that country where the sun could hardly reach the ground for the woods, those people wanted to know about the outside world, so I sold a newspaper on its merits.

. . . The last year we lived out at Wells Bayou, when I was thirteen or fourteen years old, I rented twenty acres on my own, on halves. Broke the ground and did it all. Mr. Hudson rented me the twenty acres of land and assigned me a mule. I used a second mule when I was rowing it up with a middle buster. The rest of the crop I could make with one mule. His name was Jim, and he was the worst, stubborn, no account mule in the world, and he and I got along fine. I hated him and he hated me. It really was a love/hate affair because he would come to me of a morning when I would go to the lot and nearly stick his head in the bridle. As soon as I got on him he would start bucking. But after three or four jumps he'd get settled down, and we'd go on. I had to hire help in my chopping. I had furnish just like I was forty years old so I had something coming in. I made twelve or fifteen bales and had to have pickers and used the seed money to pay the pickers. I hauled my cotton to Gould. I'd take a wagonload of cotton, about fifteen hundred pounds, and I'd leave about sundown and have to stay with it nearly all night because it would be well after midnight before it got ginned. You were always in a line at the gin, and you'd sleep and the mules would move up in the line by themselves when the wagon in front of them moved, and you woke up when your time came. Then you went home, and it was probably ten miles or so back home. I made a very good crop—only cotton. I guess I was like all other sharecroppers in the world: no matter what you made, you broke even, if you were lucky. I did not make a dime.

When I moved to Dumas, I was about fifteen, and my first job was at the ice house. That would have been about 1943. I drove a truck down to McGehee, a ton and a half truck with no brakes on it. It had big tall sideboards, and you could get thirty-six three-hundred-pound cakes of ice on that truck. I'd back the truck up to the dock, and it was a little bit lower than the dock. So the way you got it on the truck was that when the ice came out of the tank where it was frozen they scored it with a scoring machine on a belt that shot it out, and you caught it with your tongs and guided it onto the truck, thirty-six cakes, three hundred pounds apiece. Then you put a tarp on top of the load, and that kept the wind off. By the time you sold it in Dumas a fifty pound cake probably weighed forty pounds. It was a tough, tough job because we had to be down there at midnight or whenever. And sometimes I would have to wait a while to get my money. Sometimes even, Mama had to get behind the owner to get my money.

After that I went to work in a grocery store and ended up working at every grocery store in town. And finally in my senior year I worked at Kroger, and when I graduated, I went with Kroger before I started my other career.

But what I wanted to be all that time was a lawyer or an actor or a Methodist preacher but there was no way. Back in those days it couldn't work the way it can today. Anybody can go to university now, but for me it wasn't possible. I had my mother and little brother to help support.

Billy Lee Riley

The first thing I remember about [plowing at the age of ten] was the aroma, the very nice aroma, you following the mules all day. But it was beautiful. The smell of that land, that new land turning over was great. But what it was, we would first take what you call a turning plow, a plow pulled by two mules, and you would take one row at a time. It would actually turn the dirt upside down. And my brother would be following me doing the same thing, or he would be in front, and we would be doing this, we had twenty-five acres of cotton land, and it just took forever to do it. We would spend ten or twelve hours a day doing it. Then we would take this little riding disc, and we only had one of those, and we would fight over who was going to get to ride, then we would go over the land with that, and then we would take a harrow and smooth it all off, get the clods out, then we had what you call a two-row hopper, and you'd sit on a little seat and it had little hoppers filled with cotton seed, and one guy would be planting while the other would be waiting on the end to fill up those hoppers, and then we would put fertilizer down the same way. And then we would wait for cotton to sprout, and when it got about two inches high, we would get out there and chop it and thin the cotton. We would chop it twice while it was growing and a third time when it was about two feet high. You chop it and go through it and get all the weeds, and then you run the middles with this cultivator which we'd been using to plow the cotton. After we'd run the middles, the farming was over until harvest time. So it was a big job. It's easy to talk about it, but to do it takes a lot of hard work, and just getting out at daylight and harnessing up those mules was a job. (310)

. . . When you pick cotton, when those bolls open up, they become real hard, and each little part has a sharp needle point right on the end. And if you don't know how to get in there and get that cotton, your hands will just be torn up. And usually at the first part of the year, everyone's hands are cut up. Once you've learned how to get in there and get that cotton, you could do it, and it wouldn't hurt you. But it was hard on your back, the hardest work, I believe, I've ever done. You get an eight or nine-foot sack, and you go to the end of the row and take two rows back and crawl on your knees, and you're pulling the sack, and every time you get a handful of cotton in there it gets heavier. And you do it until it gets so full, and you put it on your back, and you walk to the scales and they weigh it, put it on the book, and you go back and do it again. It's something I wouldn't want to see my children have to do, but I wouldn't mind having to do it again. (310, 303)

Joycelyn Elders

I ended up with four brothers and three sisters, so there were eight of us, and I was number one. . . . If my mother went to the fields to help work, she could really keep the workers working better than I could. . . . I was the babysitter. In fact, I was kind of the mother for the rest, for my sisters and brothers. And I would stay home and baby sit and take care of the garden and cook . . . so supper would be ready. . . . I picked—I was very proud when I was able to pick 200 pounds a day. . . . We worked very hard. You know, we always really wanted to get it picked and get everything done so we could go to school. (16, 18)

Levon Helm

Waterboy! Hey *waterboy!*

That's my cue. It's harvesttime, 1947, and I'm the seven-year-old waterboy on my daddy Diamond Helm's cotton farm near Turkey Scratch, Arkansas. My dad and mom are working in the fields along with neighbors and black sharecropping families like the Tillmans and some migrant laborers we'd hired, seasonals up from Mexico. My older sister, Modena, is back home watching my younger sister, Linda, and my baby brother, Wheeler. Since I'm still too young for Diamond to sit me on the tractor, my job is to keep everyone hydrated. I got a couple of metal pails, and I work that hand pump until the water runs clear and cold. I run back and forth between the pump house and the turn row, where the people drink their fill under a shady tree limb. I learned early on that the human body is a water-cooled engine.

It was hard work. The temperature was usually around a hundred degrees that time of year. But that's how I started out, carrying water to relieve the scorching thirst that comes from picking cotton in the heat and rich delta dust.

All of us—black people, white people, Mexicans—worked together in the fields. Our family worked side by side with the Tillmans, black neighbors who were important members of our little farm community. Our families were so close that Sam Tillman gave me a spanking when I needed it. My mother might cook dinner for as many as six or eight people working in the fields. If we had a truckload of Mexicans, Dad would round them up and take' em to the grocery store or bring in bread, cheese, sandwich meat, some cold Pepsi-Colas, and maybe some apples. Then he'd gas up the tractor while we found some shade in the tree brakes. The older I got, the more I enjoyed those shade trees. (13, 28–29)

Bill Covey

b. 1935, Yell County, grew up near Watson in Desha County. Retired army officer. Interview with Margaret Bolsterli, 2009.

When you were chopping for pay, it was ten hour days, and up until I was thirteen or fourteen, I was getting half-pay. And that was fifteen cents an hour six days a week, so I would have an eighteen-dollar payday at the end of the week. You had six ten-hour days at fifteen cents an hour. But I never felt sorry for myself, and I can't say I ever knew anybody who did. Your neck would hurt so bad you could hardly stand it, and I had rather pick it than chop it because you could set your own wages. You got paid for the amount you picked, not for the hours you worked. I could pick between 250 and 300 pounds of cotton a day.

We used to have real fun picking. My dad would sprinkle tomato seeds and watermelon and cantaloupe seeds in the cotton planter then when time came to pick, on every row you'd come across watermelons and cantaloupes and tomatoes and that was kind of a bonus. People would lay them on their sacks. And people talked and told stories while picking. And they sang, especially the black pickers. Somebody on one end would start and someone way back would pitch in and then everybody in between. It was some of the best music you would ever hear. It was like being in the middle of a choir. I don't recall the white pickers ever doing that. The whites and the blacks got along out there in the field. Sadly, because I don't believe in this and hate to say it, but it was said they knew what their place was and stayed in it.

A pickup truck was the main means of transportation. I must have been ten or twelve years old when I started driving. I started hauling cotton to the gin when I couldn't have been more than twelve years old. You would go to sleep in the line, and somebody would beat on the door and wake you up to move forward. And you did that until your cotton was sucked off the truck. And then you would go home and go to school the next day. Normally you would take a bale on the pickup and then two more on a trailer.

When I was about eighteen, I decided I would rather do the manual of arms than manual farm labor, so I joined the army and stayed twenty-two years.

Grif Stockley

The summer that I was fourteen Daddy called up his cousins over near Wilson and asked if they would let me come live there, so I lived that summer with my aunt Elizabeth, "Diddy," and her son Sam. This would have been around 1958. They had a plantation, so I lived over there and carried water to the cotton choppers and learned real quickly that I didn't want to be a farmer because it was way too much work.

We got up at 4:30 and went to the commissary. They brought over cotton choppers from Memphis who would wait 'til they were out in the middle of the field and holler "water." They didn't really need it, but they knew I would have to come out there and carry those buckets. The choppers would start at seven and stop at twelve, and we would all eat dinner which was the main meal of the day. At the big house my aunt would have corn and tomatoes and chicken and beef. Of course it made me so sleepy I don't know how I made it to go back out to the field. Then when it rained, you'd think maybe they were going to slow down, but we'd have to go work on the books at the commissary. And the one night we would do anything, we would take Horace's wife into Osceola to play bridge. And we'd go to a movie, but after about twenty minutes we would go to sleep. It was a long summer, but I grew to appreciate people who farmed—and my cousins were good farmers. . . . I loved those people, but I sure wasn't cut out to work as hard as they did. This was not one of those gentleman-farmer type operations. They opened the commissary and sold the salt meat, and that summer they tolerated me. I think I made thirty dollars a week.

Helen Pennington

**b. 1946, near Watson in rural Desha County.
Retired insurance agent. Interview with Margaret Bolsterli, 2009.**

My parents were farmers. My grandpa sharecropped, and my dad and uncle did too 'til they bought land in 1947. My parents bought sixty acres and then close to another forty. There were eight children; I was the fourth child, and we were poor but we didn't know it. When I was very young, we had cows, and it was my obligation to fetch the cows in the afternoon for milking. We had our own butter. I'd wake up almost every morning hearing my daddy churning the butter, and there's nothing tastes as good as fresh churned butter over some hot biscuits. We raised most of our food, had a big garden and canned, and later on we had a freezer and we slaughtered our own pigs but seldom had beef. When we would have butcher day, my uncles and cousins would come.

Everybody else was the same as us. I didn't know I was poor until later. It must have been after I was grown. Most of the children in school were farmers also, and all my relatives were like us. There were a few people who lived in the town of Watson, where I went to school for twelve years, who owned a store, and their clothes were better than ours but so what! Most people were like we were.

When we were picking cotton, we didn't care for it. It's just what everybody did. One thing I'll never forget, the man who owned the land across the road from us lived in Dumas but had a farm manager out there with a paycheck so that family didn't pick and chop cotton. So we'd chop up the row, and there his daughter would be sitting on the porch. And we'd chop back down the row, and his daughter would still be there, sitting on the porch. And I just didn't think it was right.

We talked out there in the cotton patch and gossiped about that person sitting up there on the porch and others who didn't have to chop cotton. We made plans and we talked about what we were going to do when we got away from there and what would happen if we would suddenly get a million dollars, and we would really show these people who didn't have to work, when all of a sudden we would have something.

And also, when you get to be a teenager and you are out there chopping cotton with people your age you've known all your life, you talked about romance and flirted and stuff like that. I remember one time I was able to buy myself a little transistor radio. It was when Nat King Cole was singing "Rambling Rose," and I just loved that little radio. I would put it on the back of my sack as I was picking.

We picked cotton and chopped cotton, and I know people that were poorer than us, even. And they don't want to admit that they've picked cotton, now that they've come up in the world, but I picked cotton and I'm not ashamed of that. It made me who I am today. Everybody I knew picked cotton, except the people that lived in town. That's what we did. We wanted to eat.

Jeannie Whayne

I tried a couple of times to earn some extra money when I was about thirteen or fourteen picking some cotton, which I didn't like very much and didn't make much money at it. It was hot and you had to carry that sack and wear the gloves to keep the cotton boll pricks from scratching, and still your hands got scratched up anyway. Mostly the effort wasn't worth the amount of money you got, and it didn't take much for me to figure that out. Once in the dead heat of the summer, because my girlfriends were doing it, I decided to chop cotton too for twelve hour days, and I was paid twenty-five cents an hour. I did it for about two weeks. I would come in and be so tired at six or seven o'clock I'd just fall into bed. It was just so hot. Actually, it was a great experience for me because I wouldn't have known what that kind of labor was like if I hadn't done that. And of course I had the choice to back off of it. There wasn't any other way to make money. There weren't any other jobs.

I married between tenth and eleventh grades, a sweet little boy, and we couldn't find any work. He wanted to go to the junior college in Beebe, and I wanted to finish high school. So we worked on this dairy farm. Twice a day, seven days a week we milked the cows. Got up at four in the morning. We had one weekend off in the two years we did this. It was very good for me; there were parts of it I liked a lot. It gave me a sense of myself controlling my own fate. We got paid a hundred and fifty dollars a month, and we got the house too. When we got married, we had absolutely nothing. His parents and mine too were going through economic crises and couldn't help us. The first two weeks we were out there, there was a potato field across the road, and the farmer had told us we could have all the potatoes we wanted. And he noticed we were eating a lot of potatoes and figured out that we didn't have any money and couldn't buy any food, so he took us down to this little grocery store and set us up to buy groceries on credit. We had a limit of twenty-five dollars for food, and that's what we ate. Somehow or another we did it. A hundred and fifty dollars even then didn't go very far. I also worked in the school cafeteria during my study hall. I managed to make good enough grades to stay in Beta Club.

I remember that the people at the school thought I must be pregnant or I wouldn't have gotten married, so I had to be examined by a doctor. So I went to see the doctor and he said, "Well, tell me, girl, are you pregnant?" and I said, "No, sir." And he said, "OK," and that was my examination. I was the first married teenager who went to Beebe High School.

Karen Rudolph Shoffner

We always worked in the summer. My father, a university professor, had the attitude that he didn't get paid in the summer so neither should we, so allowances got cut, and there was a lot you had to buy. By the time I was in the seventh grade we got a clothing allowance of two hundred dollars a year, and that included shoes, coats, whatever else you had to have. Aside from that you either earned the money or made the clothes. You could buy fabric to make a dress. From the summer of the seventh grade I worked for the elderly couple across the road. I cleaned the house for them for fifty cents an hour. Then not long after that I started babysitting. The community was perfect for that. I babysat mostly for English Department faculty kids also at fifty cents an hour. And one summer I picked up some kids from across the street and tutored one who was having trouble reading. In the summer you'd busy yourself doing that kind of stuff. We certainly weren't poor.

My summers as a teenager were colored by the fact that my mother was gone every summer working on a graduate degree, so I did the cooking and laundry. There was a cleaning lady one day a week so we didn't have to do heavy cleaning, but when my parents were going to entertain, we had to dust.

Janis Faye Kearney

b. 1953, rural Lincoln County, near Gould.
Writer, publisher, personal diarist to President Bill Clinton.
From *Cotton Field of Dreams*.

Until I was seven, my life pretty much mirrored that of other poor children I knew. In 1960, things changed dramatically when I was inducted into the world of Daddy's cotton field. At seven, I became one more field hand responsible for helping my father produce his yearly cotton crops. Like my siblings, I entered into an unwritten 10-year service contract that ended when a child graduated from high school and went on to college or started life independent of the Kearney household.

. . . Like my brothers and sisters, I had a responsibility to contribute to the household, and the cotton field was how we made our contributions. There was a certain excitement about all of this—an anxiety about joining my older siblings leaving home early on summer mornings and returning late in the evenings. I anticipated joining them as they sat down together for breakfast in the mornings, and I looked forward to participating in the jokes and laughter that filled the air after their day in the cotton field. I was convinced it was something about their day in the field that produced such joy.

On my first day as a field hand I woke early. Hurrying to the front room, I heard my parents' voices and found Daddy already dressed, ready for the day's work. He looked over at me and smiled, continuing to sip his morning coffee.

"You ready to chop some cotton this morning?"

I smiled back and said, "Yeah, do I have my own hoe?"

My father nodded and said I did. Without knowing what the term meant, somewhere in the recesses of my being I understood that I was undertaking a rite of passage. After anxiously eating breakfast with the rest of the family, I heard Daddy hollering my name from the back yard. Mama smiled at me and nodded for me to go on out back.

As I waited anxiously for the day to start, my siblings walked out to the back yard, claiming their individual chopping hoes. They all gave me either a giggle or a smile. One or two told harmless jokes about this new turn in my life. As they started down the gravel road toward the cotton field, I followed. I walked fast, taking long steps to keep up with them as we trekked the half-mile to the field.

. . . "Do we have to chop all this cotton today, Daddy?" I asked, looking down the long cotton rows that stretched as far as I could see.

"No, Faye. We just chop until it's time to go home. Wherever we stop is where we start the next day."

. . . Daddy crouched down on the ground beside the small plants and pointed out which plants were weeds and which were cotton.

"You want to chop all the weeds with your hoe. The blade is sharp so you can cut it easily. Be careful not to cut yourself, though."

He pulled up the weeds, leaving one small plant standing alone. As he threw the weeds down, he looked up at me. "This here is what a cotton plant looks like." He held the plant delicately between his fingers. "You don't ever want to chop down a cotton plant 'cause that's what grows and turns into the cotton we take to the gin in the winter."

I nodded. I knew Daddy took wagons loaded with fluffy white cotton to the gin and came back with groceries and money.

. . . By quitting time that evening, I had earned my stripes, chopping several rows of cotton all by myself. The reality of what my days would be like was fast setting in. The sun's relentless heat and glare, now directly overhead, began to burn through my thick plaits and into my scalp. Daddy's raggedy old shirt had been wet with sweat, then dried by the hot sun more than once that day. The sun was unrelenting—the only reprieve being the few clouds that passed under it, offering us moments of shade throughout the day.

To get through the summers I spent in Daddy's cotton fields, I learned the trick of transposing myself to another place and time as I worked. In my mind, I might be anywhere other than the cotton field. These moments of daydreaming helped me make it through the worst days of summer. In later years when my siblings spoke with a deep hate of these summers, I'd smile and shrug, saying, "They really weren't that bad." None of them understood. (48–51)

Lillie Mae Fears

b. 1962, Chicago, grew up in Monroe and Phillips Counties. Professor. Interview with Margaret Bolsterli, 2009.

I was in Chicago for kindergarten and first grade. When we first moved to the South, my mother was a school teacher, so second and third grade were in Clarendon, in Monroe County. And then I guess around 1971, we built a house in Phillips County on the family property, and we have been there ever since.

My grandparents had a big vegetable patch, and what they would do, they would sit up, we'd stay up 'til all hours of the night, and we'd shell peas: purple hull, whippoorwill, crowder, ladypeas, butter beans, speckled beans. My grandmother had the works. We would shell them, and she would spread them out. And she would put them in different sacks, and there were always grandkids who would take turns going peddling. She would take two. My partner was my aunt who was a year older, and we would go into Helena and sell vegetables to people who lived in these big historic homes. My grandparents and the two grandkids would go from house to house, and she had a quart jar and a pint jar, and we would ask the people what they wanted. They knew she would be coming in her little blue truck, and we would just peddle. We had other kinds of vegetables too.

I remember working in the fields when you got big enough. We didn't have to work for other farmers chopping crops; we had our own crops or our grandparents' crops. And they would load us up in the back of a truck, and we'd take a keg of water, and we would leave about eight in the morning and stay 'til right at noon. And we would chop on the property in what was called the Calico Bottoms. I think that was my great-grandparents' property that they had left their four kids. So my granddad was the only one of the four children who continued to farm, and we would go chop soybeans, and then we would chop cotton on the property near the houses. We'd take turns getting the water. When I got older, I decided it wasn't really necessary to do all that chopping, but I think my dad wanted to teach us what it meant to farm, to work, because they had these tractors. The giveaway was the cotton crop because he would have us pick the ends of the rows for twelve feet, and it would take me all day to get a hundred pounds! He would tell us about how he and his brothers picked three hundred pounds a day. He'd say he needed us to pick those rows at the ends so the big cotton picker had somewhere to turn around, and as I got older, I wondered if he made that up. Turn around? There was a row that you drove on! So I wonder if he didn't just want to give us something to do, get us out of the house, teach us how to work. It sticks to you, that work ethic. My dad was a perfectionist, and he was never a wealthy farmer, but his crops were the best. I think he just liked working for himself, leaving the factories in Chicago. It meant a lot to him to work the family farm. My hobby in high school was planting a garden. I had beans and squash and okra.

When we were working in the field, we talked, argued, sang. A lot of Michael Jackson songs were popular in those days, and I remember going home for lunch breaks and sitting by the radio, and one of his songs would be on. Everybody had a buddy. My grandma had thirteen kids, and her last ones overlapped with grandkids, so her baby is a year older than I am. That was my buddy. But we knew it was work; it wasn't fun talk, as I remember. We'd be glad to get out of there and go inside, but we knew that was our chore, to get up and go to the field. Lunch was very light, usually it was bologna, just something to tide you over, and in the evening there would usually be some fresh peas and cornbread and fried chicken or such. We didn't work as hard as the people who would get on a truck and go and work for some big farmer. We did it family style. There was one weed the pesticide wouldn't kill, and it grew like a vine. And my grandmother would say it was choking the cotton, so you had to get in there and pull it out by hand.

Michael Thomas

We were pretty poor, and I had to get a job. I was a busboy and then a cook at a restaurant my junior and senior years in high school. We had a progam at school. . . . I got out at 12:30 to go to work; I always kind of hated that. It was as if school ended a little too early for me. I wanted to be at school. . . . But I enjoyed working. I was a good busboy and went right up to cook. But I didn't like the responsibility and went back to being busboy.

CHAPTER 4

School and Memory

School is a major component of the collective memory. Until well into the twentieth century, getting an education beyond the eighth grade could not be taken for granted in rural Arkansas. Because of mud, roads were usually impassible for much of the winter, and most could not afford to board in towns to go to high school. Rural schools usually had one or two rooms and were taught by one or two teachers, but those schools, with the church, provided the center for the community, and everyone took an interest in them. Schools competed in mathematics and spelling as well as basketball and baseball, so spelling bees and ciphering matches and school plays could draw an audience from miles around. The teacher either commanded respect or was dismissed. However, once gained, respect for the teacher was such that parental support was usually absolute; punishment for misbehavior at school was often repeated at home.

Getting to school was difficult and treacherous. Some children walked miles, some rode horse back, and well into the 1940s some went in covered wagons pulled by mules.

Rural schoolyards usually had no playground equipment except, sometimes, a basketball hoop and a baseball. Children played games like red rover, hopscotch, jacks, marbles, jump rope, and jumping the board. Lacking anything better to do, if there were no teachers on the playground, they would choose sides and fight. Urban schools had more amenities like libraries and playground equipment, but aside from the few larger cities, not many.

And yet most of the memories of school are sweet. People remember the thrill of learning, and they recall fondly the people who taught them. Many regret the lack of opportunity for higher education and remember forever the bitter pain of realizing after finishing the eighth grade that there would be no more formal education for them. But even they still talk with pleasure about the time they did get to spend in school.

Lily Peter

b. 1891, near Marvell, rural Phillips County.
Planter, ginner, poet. Interview with Margaret Bolsterli, 1985.

My father was a lumberman and bought thousands of acres of timberland that was terribly isolated and with no one living in that area except just a few families, maybe a half a dozen, but they were far from us and didn't share our interests at all. We had the only books, the only interest in poetry, the only interest in music. We were entirely in solitude to ourselves because nobody else shared our interests. We hardly saw anybody for the reason my father was a damnyankee. We were isolated.

. . . My parents gave me my education at home. My mother taught me my ABCs when I was two years old. When I was four or five years old, I could read all kinds of grownup books although I didn't understand them and mispronounced the words in fantastic ways. My parents used the same textbooks they had been brought up with, like McGuffey's Reader and spelling books. By the time I started going to school I could diagram practically any sentence in the English language because my mother had taught me how to do that.

When I began going to school, which I didn't begin until I was ten years old, I began Latin that summer, the summer I was ten. And bless my lucky stars I could begin it then. But I loved it. Just ate it up, and in that first long summer I was in school two months studying Latin. I memorized all five of the declensions. I memorized four of the verb declensions word for word, here in a little one-room school. Walked seven miles a day to go to school. . . . I went to that summer school two months. The next year, when I was eleven, I went to school at Turner, four miles away. I could have ridden a horse if I had wanted to, but I really preferred walking because that way I was with other children. There were so few people living back in here that I had no playmates except my brothers and sisters.

Remember, I can remember ninety years ago, and the world is completely different now. We had no high school here, even in Helena.

When I finished high school at the age of sixteen in Ohio, what I would have liked to do was impossible. I was valedictorian in my class, and I wanted to go to college more than anything else in the world, but my father was killed in a dreadful accident.

William Grant Still

I went first to Capitol Hill School, which wasn't built on a hill at all, but was located in a section named Capitol Hill. It was a school of moderate size, with a main building of red brick back of which was an old-fashioned frame structure. In the schoolyard were many rocks and trees around which were built rough benches for the children's use during lunch hours. I always ate lunch with my mother, for she taught at Capitol Hill too, but in the High School Department.

. . . Whenever I was enrolled in one of my mother's classes, such as literature, I suffered through every moment, and won the sympathy of *all* my fellow-students. Mama was determined not to let anyone accuse her of partiality; she was determined that I *had* to be a model. The slightest error found me standing in the corner, being given demerits, or feeling the sting of Mama's ruler as it cracked smartly over my fingers.

. . . Each time I was involved in a childish prank, I could count on a whipping when I got home, and I was often involved because most of my schoolmates were just as impish as I. Once, but only once, I played hookey to watch the trains pass, and to see the horses being shod in the blacksmith's shop.

Today I can find it in my heart to feel sorry for poor Professor Gillam, whom all the boys loved to torment. We poured water in his chair before he sat down; hit him in the back with little pieces of crayon when he turned around to write on the blackboard. If we had stayed in that school a few years longer we would have regretted our practical jokes, for Professor Gillam eventually became Principal and was in an ideal position to retaliate. He forgave us, though, and became a good friend in later years. (78–79)

Pearl Lou Mattmiller Katz

We walked three miles to school, and if it was raining, our father would take us in the wagon. But if the rain had frozen and the road was hard on the horses' hooves, he would not, and we would walk because his horses were not shod.

. . . We had school plays and a debating society, and on Friday afternoons very often we had speeches and recitations. We had all sorts of speeches to say. We enjoyed that work. We enjoyed having to learn something, and we enjoyed the things we had to learn in school. We enjoyed the spelling bees. We studied hard for those spelling bees. Once in a while for a worthy cause we'd have a box supper. The girls would fix the boxes and the boys would bid on them, and if they knew which boxes their girls had fixed, they would bid pretty high sometimes. They would then eat the contents of the box together.

Monroe Neal was the teacher when I started to school. And he was a big tall coarse-looking man, and I was as afraid of him as a bear, but he was just as kind and good as he could be. He was just too big and coarse looking to be a school teacher, I thought. The school had one great big room, had a wood stove, and I remember it had a stage on one end. It had two front doors and rock steps. It had metal lamp holders that hung on the wall, and you set kerosene lamps in there for lights. And then later on my granddad bought some lanterns and we used them. We didn't have a very big school.

We had spellings every Friday evening and ciphering matches. I don't remember ever missing many words. It would embarrass me to miss a word. But in the ciphering matches, I could hold my own against everybody in every encounter I ever tried but one boy. He could add two lines at once, and I couldn't do that. And he could always beat me if he came up against me because he would get to pick and he would pick addition. But if I came up against him, I could beat him because I could do division, and he just couldn't divide. Well, he could but it took him forever.

When we'd take a notion to go to Pinnacle, up there, and spell against them, Aunt Mamie, my aunt four years older than me, would say, "Let's go down to the pasture and run the horses in and we'll catch enough to ride to the school at Pinnacle." And we'd ride three or four horses up that steep hill, and you could hardly stay on coming back because we didn't have enough saddles. I know I rode behind as we went up, but they wanted me to ride in front as we came back. And I could hardly pinch my legs tight enough to stay on that horse, and it going downhill because there was about three kids behind me leaning on my back. We walked to school

We moved around so much I went to school so many places. I went to school at Good Luck and Plainview, and I went to school in Oklahoma, and I went to school at Bounty, and that's where I finished grade school. Our teacher, one of the sweetest old men that ever was, had a lodge hall up over the schoolhouse, and we made two rooms out of it. There were fourteen girls. We had two basketball teams in the school. Didn't have quite that many boys. But we studied ninth grade, and he got high school books and taught us, free of charge. And one of us kids would teach the seven grades below so he could teach us. We'd take it kind of day about. We studied agriculture, for one thing, and algebra and how to measure land. There was the Silver Burdette Eighth Grade Arithmetic book. It taught you how to paper walls and how to wrap packages, how to measure land. That was ninth grade work. We had four subjects.

I think if my mother had lived, I would have been educated, but my daddy was one of those men that thought that boys ought to be educated but women shouldn't. I wanted Dad to let me go to Uncle Noble and Aunt Mary's and stay and catch the bus to Huntsville to high school. But he said, "You don't need to go. You might turn out bad."

Phydella Hogan

I went eight years to school in the two-room school in Zion. I didn't start 'til I was in the second grade because I was so little. We lived about a mile and a half from school, and there were a lot of hills. It was a rocky road, and so they wouldn't let me start 'til I was seven. We walked. We walked everywhere. It didn't matter where you lived; there was no bus. I remember I was thrilled to death when I got to what we called the big room of the school and discovered they had what they called the library, which was nothing but *The Book of Knowledge*. That's all it was; nothing else. But it was an education in itself.

I couldn't go to high school in Springdale or Fayetteville unless I boarded there, and that's why I didn't get to go to high school. When I knew I wouldn't get to go, I cried for weeks. I even tried to get a job in town, but people just laughed at me. I was so little I looked about twelve, but I was really fourteen. It hurt. Later I taught myself shorthand and typing and bookkeeping by correspondence. I took a newspaper writing course and a short-story course by correspondence. I've read all my life. And after I came back from California, I finally started at the University of Arkansas at age sixty-seven and finished at age seventy-two, *cum laude.* Girl, we had us a party when I got through!

LaVerne Feaster

My dad took care of the plantation store, and my mother was the teacher. It was a one-room school held in the church, in the place where the deacons met and that kind of thing. Had blackboards up on the wall, and that's where they had school. Of course they only had school like December, January, February, and maybe a little of March, and then they were out for chopping until June when they went back to school for June, July, and August, and then they were out for picking cotton.

I feel sorry for the kids today because the teachers don't have the opportunity to guide and help children like they did us. My mother would bring girls home from school, and she would tell somebody, "You tell Miss Sally I took Jeannie home with me tonight." Mama would bring her home and put one of her robes on her and wash her clothes and wash her hair and straighten it and get her ready for the next day to go to school. If a teacher would do that today, there would be an uproar. There was tremendous respect for my mother.

I went to the Arkadelphia Cotton Plant Academy. It was a Presbyterian school for African American children. They had some first-through eighth-grade schools on various farms, but that was the only high school in Cotton Plant for African Americans. And it was really the only one in that area because black kids from Forrest City and Helena and all the other places up in that area came to it.

We had a girls' dormitory and a boys' dormitory, a library, and a classroom building. We had a dining room, and up over that was the home-economics building. There were apartments for the faculty. All were African Americans. We had to take turns helping in the kitchen and with the dining room, washing dishes and waiting tables and going in the kitchen to help cook. We had to take turns working in the laundry. We finally got washing machines, but I can remember when we had to rub clothes. We had to pump the water. The boys had to cut the lawn and do the outside work.

We would have parties in the cafeteria. They would push the tables out of the way, and we would dance. The teachers would all be sitting around, and if you danced too close, they made you stop. The boys would come to the girls' dormitory and pick up their dates, and the teachers would be sitting there in the hall watching us when we came downstairs to see if we were dressed properly, and if we weren't, we'd have to go back upstairs and put on the right clothes.

And of course we all had to learn how to play the piano. Most of us didn't learn well, but we had to learn some and, we had recitals where we had to play our pieces.

It was a wonderful school. You couldn't stay in the dormitory until you were in the third grade. And my brother was a grade ahead of me, and before I got to the third grade, we lived with my grandmother who lived in Cotton Plant and went to school. And then when I got to be third grade and he was fourth grade, we moved into the dormitory. And we stayed in the dormitory until we graduated from high school. It was something. There were kids from everywhere, Arkadelphia, Monticello, Camden, Morrillton, Wynne. Kids from those places would come to the academy for school. Many of them went later to Presbyterian colleges. My brother went to Johnson C. Smith, an all-boys college in Charlotte, North Carolina. When I graduated from high school, I was supposed to go to the all-girls part of Johnson C. Smith, but I told my mother he'd been bossing me all my life and I would not go to where he would be telling me what to do. So Miss Dorothy Foster, one of the teachers, said there's another Presbyterian school in Rogersville, Tennessee, and I'll take you over there. And she helped my mother and me pack my suitcase and trunk and put us on the bus and carried me to Swift Junior College in Rogersville, Tennessee. We rode the bus to Memphis and then caught the train and rode through Mississippi and Tennessee to Knoxville, and Rogersville was right outside Knoxville. It was a junior college and just like high school because it was, of course, a Presbyterian school. We had to help do the work.

William H. Bowen

Life was not all fun and games for us, though. The Altheimer School, under the direction of Ms. Ruth Suits, educated and disciplined all of us and instilled in us a sense of belonging. Determined that Altheimer's children receive a full education, she took a personal interest in each child's welfare. . . . Under Ms. Suit's leadership, the Altheimer School thrived. Latin and English grammar were taught to the point that an Altheimer High graduate could regularly test out of freshman English at Arkansas's four-year colleges. She never failed to earn the school an "A" rating among the state's then more numerous school districts. Every Wednesday morning, we had a school wide assembly in the auditorium. Ruth Suits led the student body in prayer and the national anthem, and made announcements. She stood like a Marine sergeant—erect, shoulders back, head up—and her stentorian voice reverberated throughout the building. (9–10)

Gerald Bennett

We had to carry water to the school about a quarter of a mile from a spring. I was thirsty 90 percent of the time in school. I'd sit there starving to death for a drink of water because there wasn't any back there in the bucket. And one day on the way to get water we passed some guys making shingles, sawing through this big beautiful tree. We wanted to saw it too, and these men got a kick out of that and let us. There were four boys sent at a time to carry four buckets of water back. Another boy and I started sawing, and he got tired and another took over, and I sawed every one of them down. I was always proud of that. I never did like to be beat. If I play a game, I play to win.

Fritz Hudson

In 1935, I caught the first school bus Dumas had. It was a 1935 half-ton Chevy truck with a wooden body; it had board seats with no cushions, four rows with a board down the middle as a back rest, boys on one side, girls on the other, which did not last long. When the road got a big hole in it near town, they had two busses by then and we left ours on our side of the hole and walked around it to the other bus for the rest of the trip to school. This made us late so we were marked "tardy" on our report cards.

Raymond Riggins

In the beginning I went to school at Watson and caught a bus, the bus being a covered wagon.

Then we moved and I went through the eighth grade out at Wells Bayou and started the ninth in Dumas. I have some fond memories from out there at Wells Bayou School. I remember that we boys all smoked, and when the bell rang, we'd run to the outhouse and everybody would light up a cigarette. And one day Mr. Eastham, the teacher, met us at the door. There were eight of us, and he had his yardstick in his hand and started to whip everybody. I was the last one and I was his pet, and when he got to me he said, "Raymond, I know you were out there trying to get the rest of them to come in," and I said, "Yessir, I was." I didn't get a whipping but those old boys were tough on me for a few days!

Mr. Eastham had a long bench at the front of the room, and everybody in the class he was teaching could sit on that bench. He made you parse every sentence, identify every verb and noun and everything, and I learned more from him than I did from any other teacher I had except for another good one in high school in Dumas, Mrs. Lois Haller. I can't speak any other language, but I can read a newspaper in several other languages. I have been in many other countries, and I can read their newspapers only because I had Latin with Mrs. Haller in high school. From those two teachers I learned more that put me in good stead for my career in speaking and working and everything else than I did from anybody else. Wells Bayou School was a wonderful experience, and, of course, Dumas High School was too.

Mr. Eastham always told me, "Raymond, you're better than you are. You're better than you are." And it gave me drive.

Joycelyn Elders

About before I started to school—my mother wanted to make sure that I did well when I went to school. I mean, she . . . only finished eighth grade. But it was important to her that we got what she called "an education." To her an education was to finish high school, since nobody had finished high school. You know, that was just not a thing that you thought about. So before I started school, what I remember most was my mom always trying to . . . [make] sure that I was learning my alphabets and my numbers and learning to read. And I mean she would drill. . . .

. . . I started to school when I was five. But when I started school I could read, knew my alphabets, could write all my ABC's, I could add. . . . We had a one-room schoolhouse and Miss Eulistine Brown was our teacher. And she had from first through the eighth grade. . . . And we were all inside. It's amazing. I remember how, somehow we were all kept busy doing something. . . . We were all always doing something or getting ready for the Christmas play, or Easter play. . . . All holidays were big days, Thanksgiving, because that's, that's all you had.

And we walked to school, which was about four or five miles through the woods, you know? But there were several other kids . . . that was doing the same thing so . . . they would always come by and I would join on with them for the walk to school.

. . . After a while they consolidated the one room schools and we went over to what they called Howard County Training School, which was a school for black kids for much of Howard County, and they were bussed into this one school. . . . We were divided by grades for the most part then. But even then, see, if we were needed in the fields or something, we, we just couldn't—we had to miss school. And in the fall, you know, you were gathering in the crops. So you had to be out of school to gather the crops. We were always, you know, ashamed to tell people that, what we were doing and what we had to do. But many kids were doing the same thing. (11–15)

Levon Helm

There was a one-room school at the Turkey Scratch church called the County Line School, with all the grades together. . . . This is where I started my education. . . . Just getting to the bus stop on the hard road could be a problem when the fields were flooded. Sometimes Mary Cavette and I would be covered in mud from our trip by wagon and mule to that bus stop. Mary would be crying and I'd be laughing. Sometimes a tractor had to pull us through a mudhole.

I loved school when I finally got to it. . . . I especially loved those school lunches, which changed every day, unusual for a little boy used to the routine of the farm. Things went pretty well for a couple of years until I hit the second grade. That's when I got put off the school bus for fighting. I don't remember the specifics but I got into it with some older kids who went to the bigger school back in Marvell. After that I walked the few miles to school for a year or so. When that old yellow bus passed me on the road, I didn't look at them and they didn't look at me. It was a standoff.

One of my most vivid memories of childhood is the sultry summer night in the late forties when they inoculated all the children for measles or diphtheria; whatever they were doing that night. O, God, that was a mess!. The kids had gotten wind of it and we were scared to death of those big glass syringes with the thick steel needles. They hung an old tarpaulin around the pump house. That was ugly. Us kids *knew* we were in trouble now. It was usually wide open, a nice place to sit and have your lunch. All of a sudden it was dusk, and the pump house was hidden by this tarpaulin lit by yellow kerosene lanterns inside. It was like a slaughterhouse, with farm folks holding the terrified children. I tried to hide out, but someone caught me and threw me in the wagon, and the mules pulled up to that pump house. It took a fight, but they eventually got us all.

We had a nice [high] school and some good teachers in Marvell, but my mind was usually elsewhere. I wanted to play music, and that's it. It didn't matter whether I was in class or driving a stinking tractor in one-hundred-degree heat after school let out in May. I knew that playing for people was a lot healthier than inhaling gasoline fumes to get high after a brutal day in the sun.

In the dark of night I'd lie in my bed and listen to the train whistles in the distance. I wanted—I needed—to go. To me the prettiest sight in the world was a '57 Cadillac rolling down the road with a doghouse bass tied to the top. That looked like the car I wanted to be in. (22, 42)

Helen Pennington

I went to school in Watson, and there were twenty-one in my graduating class. The population had started falling off. In my earlier grades we had bigger classes.

Most of the small-farm families had to miss the first six weeks of school to pick cotton. We were allowed to miss the first six weeks; we just made it up. If it rained, we would get our lessons. The teacher would tell us we had to turn this in and this in and this in, and we would turn it in. And I always made better grades after the cotton season was over, and we could go to school. I'm sure they had very small classes until the cotton was picked.

Sometimes I would get aggravated with my teacher and say I was going to quit school. My older brother and sisters had graduated, and I was expected to do it as well. And it seldom occurred to me that I wouldn't, but every now and then I would just think, "Why bother?" And Mother would just say, "All right." And then I would think, "Do I really want to pick cotton the rest of my life?" And I would stay in school.

Terry Shoffner

I went to school in Weldon for the first, second, and third grades and then was bused to Newport. My mother was my teacher for grades one, two, and three and taught all three of those grades at the same time. She then was moved to Newport when they closed the school at Weldon three years later.

At Weldon, there was playground equipment at the school. A local farmer who had a shop for repairing equipment made a big slide, built like a fortress and a big swing set—double swings with a monkey bar in the middle. There were pie suppers to raise money for things like this. We had a huge playground, several acres where we played red rover and cowboys and Indians. The old railroad bed ran through it, and there were colored stones on it that we used to collect as gold and other valuable things. We had a good time and looked forward to it. My mother, the teacher, was out there, not just on guard duty but playing with us. There was always a lot of respect for the teacher. And she was very caring. If you got a whipping in school, you probably got one when you went home too. If a teacher disciplines a child now, the parent will be at the school the next day. We had a cook who fed us lunch. There were two outdoor toilets at the back part of the property. There was no indoor plumbing until I was in grade three and no phone until I was at the university.

One year we did a Tom Thumb Wedding. I was the preacher, the boy across the street was the groom, and my cousin was the bride. I remember having to memorize a lot of lines, and there was a big crowd, and I just remember that it was a wonderful thing, a lot of fun to do. Everybody in town came, and we had relatives from Newport showing up too. The school had two big classrooms with a sliding wall between them, a dining room, and kitchen. The sliding wall was usually in place, but for that play they opened it, and there were enough people to fill all the classroom space and the dining room.

In high school, I was a little bit shy, coming from the country, but I did make a lot of friends. And in grade ten, when I began working in town, I would work until eight at night. Then I would get together with the crowd. And I remember I was a bit of an outsider, but I would get invited to parties. I guess I had a little bit of an inferiority complex, being from the country. I don't know why I would feel that way. But I did begin to mix with another crowd. I sort of broke with the Weldon kids when we started to school in Newport although we still lived close to each other. Actually when I went to the university, my roommate was from Newport, and I recall being flattered that he asked me to be his roommate.

I would guess that probably in grade ten I knew that I would leave Jackson County. My parents thought I would come back. My mother blamed herself, thinking she had done something that made me want to leave.

Martha Conner McNair

I went to elementary school in Augusta and to high school in Newport. In elementary school, we had a little bit of playground equipment, one of those poles with chains on it that you just grabbed and ran around. I remember that people would get their tongues stuck on the pole when it was cold, and they would get in trouble because you weren't supposed to put your tongue on it. But we played games like red rover and mother-may-I and Simon says and jacks and jump rope. And Hula hoops came in when I was in third or fourth grade, so we got Hula hoops. Before we could take them to school, somebody's parents bought enough for everybody to have one. Because that was a big thing: you couldn't have more, or show that you had more, than the others, or act like it. In fact, you did the reverse. I remember being seriously told not to tell what I got for my birthday or Christmas, just to say this and don't mention these other twenty-three things. It would be like bragging that you had more. You wouldn't realize that's how it would be received, and so before we could take Hula hoops to school, everybody had to get one. I remember that some had roller skates and even ice skates, but we didn't because there wasn't anywhere to roller skate. We would borrow our cousins' when we went into town. One family had ice skates because they had this little shallow pond that would freeze over maybe one time a year that they could play on, and if you fell in, it wasn't deep enough that you were in any trouble.

It was simply expected that we were going to go out and do something. There was a lot of attention paid to that. I remember that one of my best friends was Betsy Gregory, who lived in Gregory, and they went to Memphis on Saturdays for her brother to learn Latin because there wasn't anybody to teach it in Woodruff County. By the time I got that old, there was a really good teacher in Newport. That was part of the reason we moved there in addition to my mother wanting to be in a town. But people were always doing things in the summer to prepare them for college. Vanderbilt had summer programs. Southwestern, now Rhodes, had summer things that people went to because you were still pretty much dependent for teachers on who happened to move back after college, either married or unmarried, and so there wasn't much in the way of college-preparatory courses.

Randall C. Ferguson Jr.

I was in all-black schools until I was a sophomore in high school. And, Camden High School, I think, had its first black the year before I went—as I remember, there was a single black student and then the next year, I was among a group of people that went. . . . I graduated in 1970.(6)

The worst experience for me in high school—it was two. One is that even though I finished either fourth or sixth, I can't tell you which it was, in my class, I was never voted into the National Honor Society. . . . The teachers voted for that. And while I was an all-district basketball player, I never got in trouble, my last five semesters there I had all A's and one B, I was never suspended, the teachers were all nice to me [but] they never voted me into the National Honor Society.

. . . It was clear that being black, I wasn't supposed to be in the National Honor Society, even though there were fifteen honor graduates that year, and. . . . I was either fourth or sixth, I can't remember. Of the honor graduates, there was one black and that was me. The fourteen other honor graduates were all in the National Honor Society, even those I outranked. . . . So that was pretty disappointing. And that was the first time I really noticed, and said, "Wait a minute. What's going on here? I mean I'm working my butt off. I mean, how are these people getting elected into the National Honor Society and they don't even have my grades?" . . . Before that, you know, we lived in our own world. You know, things were good. I dealt with other black kids; I grew up with other black kids, and things were great.

At least for me, I thought they were great and then that happened. And it's interesting that, well, I didn't get it my sophomore year, didn't get it my junior year. I was hoping that my senior year, that that would be the year that it would happen. But . . . I had P. E. the last period of the school day. Well, I had study hall the period before and so, since I had good grades I was allowed to come over to P.E. early and there was a girls' P.E. class going on. So I would sit up in the stands doing my homework. And when they went to get dressed, which was maybe, fifteen-twenty minutes before the bell rang, then

I went and put on my basketball practice stuff and then I came out and shot baskets, getting ready for the last period.

Unbeknownst to me, the girls that were watching me went back to study hall and one of em passed a note to the other one, that got intercepted that said, "I love Randall Ferguson." . . . Now, I don't know any of them. I got called to the principal's office, and they want to know if I knew some young lady. I said, "No, I don't. I don't know her." They said, "Are you sure?" I said, "I mean I'm positive. I don't, don't know her." Then they told me she was a freshman; I'm a senior. I said, " I do not know her." And I remember finally saying—he kept asking me as if he didn't believe me, and this was the principal—never will forget—and I told him I didn't know her, didn't know what he was talking about, but, I mean if—if I *had*, what's the big deal?" And he looked at me—I'll never forget, he looked at me and said, " I thought you were one of the good ones." He said, "You can go on back. I thought you were one of the *good* ones."

I mean, I was the good—I've got straight A's, well behaved, all-district basketball player. . . . But I never got in trouble. . . . That was the only thing that ever happened. And I remember meeting the young lady and her telling me, "I want you to know that the principal just called me into his office, and he wanted me to know that you did not make the National Honor Society again, and I'm the reason why."

I don't think I ever told my parents this story, actually. But those were the two—and those two things sort of made me work even harder. It didn't make me say, "Well I worked my butt off in high school, obviously nothing good is going to come from working hard." (30–34)

Janis Faye Kearney

[The Kearney children had to pick cotton for the first three months of the school year but they were allowed to attend the first week of school to get their assignments.]

During those days, we collected our books and the instructors' guidance sheets to serve as our maps for the rest of the semester, whether we were sitting in the classroom or not.

. . . The Kearney children's education was a family affair. During fall evenings after we'd eaten Mama's dinner and cleared the table of dishes, we gathered there for our daily study sessions. . . . Priority No. 1 during our autumn days was Daddy's 50 acres of rented cotton fields. The number of bales of cotton we helped Daddy produce had direct correlations to how well we lived and ate that winter. The soft, white stuff subsidized our existence—the food we ate and the clothing we wore for the rest of the year.

It was the nights, however, that the Kearney children loved most. Our nights were dedicated to feeding our minds. While Daddy was convinced the combination of hard work and strong intellect would serve us well for years to come, for us those evenings around the dinner table with our books and paper were simply wonderful respites from our harsh, everyday realities. Beyond the inherent joy we gained from learning was the realization that using our mind(s) meant we were more than just another field hand in Daddy's and the white farmers' fields.

. . . To James and Ethel Kearney's credit, we took to learning like tadpoles to muddy bayou water. It seemed that each successive child learned earlier than the one before. We scoured Daddy's well-worn Bibles, milk cartons, oatmeal boxes, the few precious books in the house or the four-page *Lincoln Ledger* newspaper that Daddy picked up in Star City. We settled to our nightly homework sessions shortly after dinner—the only time the Kearney household experienced complete quiet, except when we slept. The only sounds in the house at those times were the scraping of our pencils on the thin, lined sheets of paper and quiet mumbling as we read the night's lessons to ourselves or some child asking Daddy a question about something he might know the answer to. (158, 161)

Julie Gabel

I went to Leverett Elementary and lived on Hall Avenue, so I could walk to school. Started first grade in 1964. I loved elementary school, and I loved my teachers. I loved to read. My sixth-grade teacher was Mrs. Keesee, and she really got me excited about books. . . . I liked school so much, in fact, if I could make money going to school I'd probably still be going.

I was very involved in music by the time I got to high school. I had learned that I had a talent for singing and started taking voice lessons from one of the university professors when I was fourteen or fifteen. So I was singing in choirs. I also took gymnastics and ballet lessons and had a lot of extra curriculars. . . . I enjoyed high school. My senior year I was a bit bored because I didn't need many credits, and so didn't have many classes.

I still love big-band music, and my dad played it all the time. There were albums that I knew every word of every song . . . and my production company just did a Christmas play over at the UArk Ballroom, and in some of the scene-change music and pre-show music I used some of the songs from some of my Christmas albums when I was a kid, the Ray Conniff Singers. And one of the women in my cast said, "What is that music from? I love it!" And so I got her that CD because she liked it so much. I just loved the whole night club scene: Rosemary Clooney and that soft, soulful music when I was very young. And then when I was in junior high, I played the violin and really loved classical music, and John Denver, for some reason. I was into classical music. I had a poster of Beethoven over my bed and loved Schubert and Tchaikovsky and Chopin. Beethoven especially.

The Doobie Brothers were my very first rock concert that I got to go to, at Barnhill, and I remember that I really didn't enjoy it very much. It was so loud! There was marijuana in the air so thick you could hardly breathe. I thought, "Oh my gosh! You could get stoned just sitting here."

I liked some of the pop music and learned all that and that was in the days of disco. And I enjoyed it all, but the albums I would buy would be more classical. When I was twelve or thirteen, I had a good girlfriend, and she played the French horn. And we lived kind of close, and she and I would walk up to the concert hall at the university. The concerts were free, and we would just go to concerts, you know, a lot. Sometimes, we would take our instruments outside and tack our music up on a tree and play outside, sometimes in my front yard or her back yard and once or twice on the university campus. Most of my friends didn't quite get that music thing, the violin and things. But she was a good friend and did. We're still good friends.

Lillie Mae Fears

My mother was a fifth-grade teacher in Clarendon when I was in second grade. Her classroom was across the hall from my room. Her first cousin was my second-grade teacher.

By the time third grade came around, we had integration. That's when things changed a lot. They moved my mother away somewhere, and of course we left our all-black school, Carver Elementary in Clarendon, and they moved us to where the all-white school was, not too far from where we were but it was a longer walk from the house and my teacher was still a black lady, a distant cousin, an older female, an interesting lady. I think she tried to compensate for us being with white people. I remember being on the playground and at the age of eight or nine. For me it's just a matter of being every man for himself to get a swing, to get on a seesaw. And you don't know a thing about racism, and I would hear her say, "Let the white kids swing," "It's time to let the white kids swing," "Y'all, let the white kids swing." She was older. I would wonder, "Why is she saying that?" And then I started realizing the difference between being white and black because my mother and dad never talked black, white. Even when we moved down to where racial tension was a little higher in Phillips County, Mother and Daddy just never warned you about racism or anything. So I have to admit that what I learned about racial tension

I learned outside of my home. The only thing I remember my mother telling us about was the story of Emmet Till. She would scare my brother if he misbehaved. She would say, "You gonna end up like Emmet Till." And I put two and two together because I read *Ebony* and *Jet* magazines faithfully from age eight, probably ever since I could read. That was my door outside my little world. The third grade was when I started learning the differences between being black and white.

There were some other things I probably picked up on as a child. That's why I know children probably pick up more than you think they know. You may be sending out messages you might not think matter, but I know I picked up on some things. You know, little things like if you have a set of text books, this happened one time in third grade, and there are only so many new ones. And there are some old ones, and I remember just sitting there thinking, They'll probably give all the white people the new ones and they'll finish the rest with us. I don't know why I thought that. It was just something as simple as getting a textbook, and I saw that some were really crispy and new, and I thought, at eight and half or nine years old, that they'll give all those to the white kids first. I probably didn't get it from my mother, but I picked it up somewhere, probably from that teacher who said, "Let the white kids swing some." Then we moved on to Phillips County, and there was probably more about the racial tensions there, little things I would pick up on and think.

In high school I was the smart black kid. I finished in the top five in my class. I always knew I wanted to go to college. As a child in elementary school, I would read the yearbooks my aunts brought home every year. I knew the faces and names of most of the people from the University of Arkansas, Pine Bluff, that used to be AM&N, because I would sit there and read them. I knew I wanted to go to AM&N. I knew what I wanted to do. And then eventually I had aunts who went to Arkansas State University. And they would bring their yearbooks home, and I would read them. I had yearbooks that I was looking at all the way until I enrolled!

Michael Thomas

We moved from Brookside to the trailer park to Ora Drive in Fayetteville to a house I loved. And then Norman left us again and we couldn't afford the house there, so we moved to Springdale for ninth grade. I had to go to Southwest Junior High, and I hated it. It pulled me away from my good friends. The only thing that had been kind of consistent in my life was my friends. The family wasn't because of the men coming in and out of my life. The friends at school were my saving grace. By that time I had found the theater bug, loved to make people laugh. It was like I was addicted to laughter. I loved my friends, loved to make them laugh, and I just got so close to so many of them. And then I was pulled out and sent to a Springdale school. And they were different; they were country kids.

I was a new kid and had long hair, and we were poor and my jeans had patches. My mom worked in a dry cleaner's, and so she had all these clothes that people had left there that didn't really fit me right. And my jeans had patches. I remember one pair that had a Crown Royal patch on my knee from that bag that Crown Royal comes in. And she kept telling me, "College kids love these patches. College boys all wear patched-up pants." And the bell bottoms with the paisley slit, I had those. And these pants were just threadbare. And she had a shirt for me that had some Greek symbols on the pocket for a sorority. It was a Levi shirt, but it was for a girl! And I had this long hair, and it was thick and I was constantly being called a girl. So here I am in the ninth grade trying to find my identity, in a new school, and I didn't want to be there. Nobody understood me and it was horrible. I can look back now and know that I was depressed. My grades started falling. . . . I was a little chubby, had long hair and patched clothes, and it seems I was picked on.

I remember getting hit with snowballs one day, just got pelted with three or four snowballs, and it hurt. I didn't turn around; I just kept walking, and I told my mom I didn't want to go back to that school. That day, I had gone in and talked to the counselor. Somebody had squirted glue in my face in art class, and I wiped it on his jacket. And we got in a fight, and I was in the counselor's office crying. And she couldn't take my crying. I remember her saying, "You clean up that face. Don't be crying in here." She was supposed to be a counselor! She said, "Here's a box of Kleenex. You need to clean your face up," and she left, and I got up and left too. I walked out. And as I was leaving, the kids in the gym class were outside, and they threw snowballs at me as I was leaving. It was insult to injury. I wasn't going back there.

I wasn't a strong-voiced kid. I was well mannered. I wasn't going to put my foot down and say no. I wasn't that kind of kid. I thought Mom would just tell me to buck up and go back. I couldn't even make a list of all the things that were wrong with that school. I remember hypodermic needles in the bathroom, and kids would be depantsed in the bathroom. What? This had never happened in my school in Fayetteville, or I just ran with a different crowd that didn't do these kinds of things. My humor just wasn't coming across. It was as if they were laughing at me and not with me.

My mom called the Fayetteville superintendent, Harry Vandergriff, and told the story. We went in to see him, and she said she worked at the Razorback Dry Cleaners in Fayetteville and wouldn't mind dropping me off every day at school and was there any way. . . . And I will always love Harry Vandergriff, who said, "That doesn't seem like a problem. Let's get that young man back in Fayetteville schools." And we sat there in his office, and she did it! My mom dropped out of school in the eighth grade, but she got me back in that school. And my grades went back up, and I was with my friends again. It could have been my perception, but all of a sudden, the teachers were in tune with me again. They were talking to me and looking at my strengths.

So I got to finish my high school career at Fayetteville High, and I was class clown, making people laugh, and I got in trouble for that a lot. As a teenager you don't know those limits, where to stop. Mooning was a big deal. One game day, I was caught in the back of a pickup truck in front of the school, mooning everybody. Just dropped my pants in the back of this pickup, and my friend was driving and we just kept on going. Everybody was laughing at that. And then the principal, Mr. Bruner, called me in, of course. "Do you have some kind of sexual problem, do you think? For doing something like that? The other kids tell me that it's nothing for you to just drop your pants anywhere." "No, sir, I think that was just the second time I've ever done it." "Don't you know kids are laughing *at* you. They're not laughing with you." I remember saying to him, "Well, at least they're laughing."

The big thing that finally got him was that I wore my pajamas to school one time to kind of protest the dress code. There wasn't a really consistent dress code. . . . And I said it doesn't say you can't wear pajamas. So I took bets that I wouldn't wear my pajamas to school. One kid bet a dollar, this kid bet seventy-five cents, this kid bet a quarter. I had three friends be my agents and write all these bets down. It added up to like ninety dollars that I wouldn't wear my pajamas to Fayetteville High School. So on that morning I rode up on my motorcycle that Norman had bought me with backup alimony money he hadn't paid for, like, two years, . . . so I rode in my pajamas from Springdale to Fayetteville. And I was in school for the first two periods and people were laughing, the teachers were laughing, and I wasn't being a behavior problem. There was a little talk at the first of class, the teacher would say, "Mr. Thomas is in his pajamas today, I see," and they would go on. When we got to the third period the loudspeaker said, "Mr. Thomas, please come to the office." Mr. Bruner had had enough. This was after the mooning experience.

He said, "You've got ten minutes to get home and change and get back here or you are out of this school." "In ten minutes? I live in Springdale." "Now you've got nine minutes and forty seconds." I remember saying to myself that he wasn't playing. But I couldn't get all the way to Springdale and back in nine minutes and twenty-nine seconds, . . . but I went home and changed and came back and he wanted to expel me, wanted Mom in there, called her. It was a big deal to call parents in. Mom cried. He went back to that thing again, "I think he's got some kind of issues, you know, that exhibitionism or something like that," and then he said *it*. Mr Bruner said *it*. He said, "Mike there's a play coming up. *A Midsummer Night's Dream* is coming up in the theater department. Do you think we could get your energies going that way?" And my cousin Grant had told me years earlier that

I should be a comedian or storyteller, but he didn't know the words for it. Mr. Bruner was the one who pushed me into it as a sophomore. He was rough. He was being a disciplinarian, but he did what I do with my students: he took my shoulders and turned me around. And I did *Midsummer Night's Dream*, one of those characters that had to dress up like a woman in the play within the play. And I had the fake grapefruits in the front, and they fell out and people roared. They cracked up, and boy, when that laughter came across the stage, I *got* it. I thought, "And I'm supposed to be doing this? I'm not getting in trouble for it!" And I was hooked. This is what I'll do. And it was Shakespeare too, that not everybody liked or liked to do. They were cracking up. I just loved it. Girls loved it. I made new friends. And that was *it*. I just wanted to make people laugh. I was really just trying to find my way. Ms Collier, Pat Collier, helped me find that venue, and Mr. Bruner.

Belle Harris Blackburn at left, feeding chickens with Williminina Alman, Rogers (Benton County), Arkansas, about 1906. *Courtesy Shiloh Museum of Ozark History (S-87-258-43)*

above: Nuckols children. Joy Nuckols Hudson holding cat. *Courtesy Joy Nuckols Hudson*

right: Roy Reed and little sister, Hattie. *Courtesy Roy Reed*

Prairie Grove Canning Company, Prairie Grove (Washington County), Arkansas, 1920s. *Courtesy Shiloh Museum of Ozark History (S-90-20)*

Sally Stockley, Martha Land, and Harriet Stockley. *Courtesy Sally Stockley Johnson*

Shirley Abbott and
her mother, Velma.
Courtesy Shirley Abbott

Ted Willis, Jodie, Robert, and Margaret Jones
(Bolsterli). *Author's collection*

Alfred Sisco and family in their garden, Osage (Carroll County), Arkansas, about 1914. *Courtesy Shiloh Museum of Ozark History/Ruth Sisco Curnutt Collection (S-85-284-80)*

Stave Mill at Bay, Arkansas. Courtesy Terry Shoffner

Terry Shoffner as preacher in Tom Thumb wedding. *Courtesy Terry Shoffner*

Wags at Stave Mill, Bay, Arkansas. *Courtesy Terry Shoffner*

Three kids on a horse, Arkansas County. *Dorothy Core Collection. MC 1380, Box 86-6, Photograph 56, Special Collections, University of Arkansas Libraries, Fayetteville*

Waiting for the art lesson in Dumas, Joy Nuckols (Hudson), Elinor Smith, Jodie McKennon, Carrie Mae Fanduward, Biddley Shea. *Courtesy Joy Nuckols Hudson*

Weighing up cotton, Mississippi County. Arkansas Giant. *MC 1780, photography 1. Special Collections, University of Arkansas Libraries, Fayetteville*

William Grant Still
and violin. *Courtesy
William Grant Still
Music. Copyright, all
rights reserved at
williamgrantstill.com*

Martha Conner
McNair, left, and
sister Ann Conner
Dillard. *Courtesy
Martha Conner
McNair*

Bill Bowen,
fall 1940.
*Courtesy Bill
Bowen*

Jeannie Whayne and her brother and greyhounds. *Courtesy Jeannie Whayne*

Kathy Mandrell
Vanlaningham and
parents. *Courtesy Kathy
Mandrell Vanlaningham*

Easter Sunday on the levee,
Helen Pennington, left
front. *Courtesy Helen
Pennington*

JoAnn and Janis Kearney, right, with visitors. *Courtesy Janis Kearney*

Delta Willis with her mother. *Courtesy Delta Willis*

Pearl Lou Mattmiller Katz. *Courtesy Joe Irby and Martha Morton*

CHAPTER 5

Play and Memory

Before television and computers and cell phones provided easy entertainment, people had to find ways to entertain themselves. Country children were especially ingenious at it.

Play in the private arena of family and home for both town and country children frequently involved nature and freedom to an extent hard to imagine today. Boys expected to hunt and fish and swim and were allowed to roam at will, within certain geographical parameters, with few warnings about danger. A surprising number of girls were taken by their fathers into the woods and taught to shoot as well. Little girls played with dolls, both real and paper, and made up appropriate scenarios like tea parties for them. At least one little girl got great pleasure from watching her mother apply makeup.

Children in towns played in the streets from sun-up until bedtime. Rural children made up their own games, such as walking the fence, in which they walked on the top of a wooden fence like walking a tightrope, and rolling tires, in which old tires took the place of hoops. When there was a group of them, they played the same games the town children played. Rural schools had little in the way of playground equipment, so in addition to baseball and basketball, frequently played on a dirt court, children played games like red rover, mother may I, hopscotch, jacks, marbles, kick the can, hide and seek, and shinny.

In some families children made up plays and acted in them. After television came, they would make up performances for talent shows and present them, serving as both performers and audience.

When there was material, children read and read and read.

Dancing was the entertainment of choice for teenagers. Some sophisticated urban areas had cotillions where preteens were taught dancing and manners. Some schools and even churches sponsored dances, but in communities where there were none provided, teenagers made do with whatever spaces they could find, including highway bridges. In communities where close dancing was frowned upon, there were play parties, where the participants square-danced and played games

Going to town on Saturday was a big event. During harvest season in the Delta, it was common for farm children to put on their best clothes, climb on top of a the newly picked bale of cotton and ride to market towns like Dumas to see and be seen and attend the movies. Similarly, kids in rural Washington and Madison Counties would go to Fayetteville and Springdale and Huntsville with their families. Adolescent girls in Little Rock would dress up and go downtown to shop with their mothers in department stores.

Pearl Lou Mattmiller Katz

We had to make our entertainment. We read and read and read. And we had play parties, and we had dances. And our cousin George and his brother-in-law made music for us, a violin and guitar. And we danced and we played "Skip to My Lou" and "Old Dan Tucker" and so on. But when we were still younger we would have an awfully good time pretending to have tea parties. We would pass little pieces of broken glass, and that was our cup of tea. So we made believe a lot. We had to stay out under the trees in the summertime to make believe when our mother was lying down to take a nap after the noon meal.

My sister Irene and I walked the fence around the cow lot. It was a big lot with a fence made of six-inch-by-one-inch boards, and we walked on that barefooted all around the lot and landed on the posts that held the big gate up alongside the road. We walked that fence and stood on those big posts and had a dialogue. I remember one time the dialogue went something like this: I was speaking about marrying a man, and my sister tried not to let me marry that man. She told all sorts of terrible things he did to try to dissuade me, and I kept saying, "Oh, but Sister, I love him," and then she would list some more of the things he did and wouldn't do. And I would say, "Oh, but Sister, I love him." I don't know how long that went on, but she never could convince me. I thought love would cure all.

Thinking about the entertainments we had, we had school plays and a debating society, and on Friday afternoons very often we had speeches and recitations. So you can see, we had a rich inheritance. We had to make our fun ourselves because it wasn't manufactured for us. Now I do not think that was a bad idea. I think it was good for us. I think our lives were enriched for us because we learned a lot of things and to do a lot of things and to enjoy everything that we did.

La Verne Feaster

I shall never forget we'd go to town on Saturday evening late. We'd be walking around, all the parents and kids, and we'd go and visit with each other. They had a barbecue stand right behind the bank and the store and sold barbecue out of windows. We couldn't go in the front of the drugstore where they sold the ice cream. Black people had to go in the back door and walk out the back door and eat our ice cream. Mama wouldn't let us walk the street eating, so we would wait until time to go home and walk in the back of the drug store and get our ice cream and come on out and get in our car and be ready to go home. And I said one time, "Mama, old Alice Mapps was sitting there on the stool eating her ice cream, and I had to get mine and come on out of the store." And she said, "What difference does it make. She's not any better than you are just because she's sitting in there eating her ice cream. That's just the way it is." Her daddy was the blacksmith on the plantation, and I would say, "My daddy's more than he is. He runs the store." One other thing I can tell you about Alice Mapps, they went to Cotton Plant to school. The bus picked them up out on the plantation and carried them to school. Black kids had split sessions, but white kids started in September and went on through May. So Alice would be going to school while Mama would be at home, and she'd get off the bus. And instead of going home, she'd come over there, and Mama would help her with her lessons.

But I never felt that I was less than any white person even though we could not do things that they could do because Mama told us, "That's just the way it is. That doesn't make you any less than they are." They taught us that light-skinned girls with better hair weren't any better than we were. We didn't feel inferior about anything.

William H. Bowen

From *The Boy From Altheimer.*

My brothers and I, along with our friends, spent much of our free time around and in the bayou. Once I helped build a flat-bottom boat so we could explore more of the area. We built the boat with great care out of used front porch flooring that was ill-suited for a boat. We put it in the bayou and it went straight down because there was not enough water displacement for it to float. I was about ten or twelve at the time, surrounded by fellow carpenters of comparable age and skill, including my brother Jim, who was about seven. Eventually, we obtained a suitable cypress boat and later, a barge, so we always had transportation through Flat Bayou. After school, my brothers and I and our friends played sports: six-man football, basketball, softball, and baseball. We also wrestled and boxed some. Our home was sort of an assembly point for all the activities. Life was not all fun and games for us, though. (7–10)

Robert E. Jones

I remember climbing trees, playing cowboys and Indians and walking the mile and a half from our house to our friends, the Irbys, to play when I was six or seven years old. Only black people lived on each side of the road all the way. We knew them all and I had no fear.

In my junior high and through high school age, we would have parties around at different places and play so-called "games" and many times would never go inside the house where the party was being given. Maybe it was a wiener roast or a marshmallow roast. But we didn't dance. And I have wondered why it didn't bother the parents for their daughters to walk across town in a small town that didn't have any street lights or down a country road in the dark but they didn't want them to dance! That may be one of the reasons I'm not a good dancer now. There didn't seem to be too much future in dancing.

Raymond Riggins

The only playground equipment at the Wells Bayou school was a dirt, outdoor basketball court, and we all played, boys and girls and everybody. I was a pretty good basketball player. I made all district when I played at Dumas High School after I learned not to allow for the wind.

Gerald Bennett

There were two places down the road that had children, and about the time the sun went down you had had your supper. The cows were milked and the wood was carried in, and these kids were either up at our house or we'd be down at theirs. We'd play hide and seek. We'd sail out of the top of the barn. I don't know how we kept from getting killed. Kick the can and ante over. For that you'd throw a ball over the house, four or five children on each side of the house, and they'd throw the ball over the house. And the ones that got it would chase the ones that didn't have it and try to knock them down with the ball. We did quite a bit of fighting. At school, we didn't have any playground equipment. We played a lot of ball. Our teacher would buy twine and make balls. Sometimes, he would put a golf ball inside to start it, and then he would wind it round. And every now and then he would sew it, and a bunch of kids could play with it half a school year. It was a good ball. You could knock it a long way.

Fritz Hudson

I remember that we always wanted to see the Friday night or Saturday ten-part serials at the movies in Dumas. The movie cost ten cents, popcorn five. There were three of us kids and times were hard. One time when the last chapter was to be shown, no money was to be had so Dad borrowed the money from a café owner for us to go while he and Mother sat in the car and waited for us.

Joy Nuckols Hudson

Some of my happiest memories occurred growing up on what is now Court Street in Dumas, at that time a dead end street. Of course there was no air-conditioning, only fans in summer, so after supper the adults would sit on their porch swings and watch the kids playing in the street. We played games like Red Rover, Tag, Hop-Scotch and Hide and Seek until we were made to come in to clean up for bed.

The nineteen thirties and forties in small-town Arkansas was a safer time. No one locked doors; kids could walk anywhere after dark. Band was introduced as an after-school activity when I was in seventh grade; Paul Wallick came from Monticello on Wednesdays to teach. I took the flute, my sister started clarinet and my brother, trombone. They were in high school and after practice they would meet their friends at the Best Café downtown and I, being only twelve years old, was delegated to carry all of our instruments home, after dark! Perfectly safe.

When Shirley Temple debuted in the movies, it was a real treat to get to see her; she was every little girl's ideal. I can remember being jealous of a classmate in first grade because she had blonde curls and her mom corkscrewed them like Shirley's. I had the basic Buster Brown shingled up the back with bangs in front. I'm still a Shirley Temple fan.

Later, when I was a bit older, we spent our Saturdays going to Meadors' Pharmacy for lunch—twenty-five cents total, sandwich-15 cents, drink-five cents, chips-5 cents, then a movie usually a Gene Autry western for ten cents and popcorn, five cents.

I was a quiet child; I read a lot—loved the Bobbsey twins and later Nancy Drew. My favorite toys were dolls; I received one every Christmas until I stopped believing in Santa Claus and I played with paper dolls non-stop, keeping each one and its clothes in a separate box. I had scads.

The United States entered the War when I was eleven; I remember going with my sister and her friends to the depot while they flirted with the GI's hanging out of the windows of the troop trains going through.

Shirley Abbott

She [mother] had a wonderful drawer of cosmetics. I think the women in her family must have yearned for such things since the dawn of time. In any case, my mother thought that makeup was one of the fine arts. She had an enormous dressing table, a yellow satin-veneer piece with a kneehole and a mirrored top, and a vast standing mirror that reflected the whole bedroom. There was a little low-backed bench and four drawers; in them she kept all her wonderful implements of beauty. Not every day, but once a week, or any time she was going out shopping, she would bathe, put on her stockings and a lacy slip and high-heeled shoes, and sit down to paint. I would abandon dog, swing, book, or any other pursuit in order to watch her. I'd come indoors and post myself beside the bench.

The open drawers gave off the most ravishing smells. Down in their depths sat little white jars with pink lids, black cylinders trimmed in silver, pink glass things with tiny roses on top, high-domed boxes with face powder inside . . . fresh powder puffs, miniature caskets with trick openings, compacts with pearl lids that shut with a glamorous click. . . . Meanwhile, I would be taking the tops off all the lipsticks and unscrewing jar lids, hoping to have a say-so in what she applied next. I liked the smoky eye shadow, the blue rouge (it was *blue*), the dark maroon lipstick, and whatever came in exotic packaging. But she seldom followed my leads. (171–72)

Helen Pennington

In addition to the eight of us in my family, my uncle and his children lived across the bayou—that's Cypress Creek. And he had nine children, and everyone caught the school bus at our house. The neighbors across the road would come, and there might be twenty children to catch the bus. There was always someone to play with, and down the road on the north side the kids would come to our house too because my mother was a good cook. We played ball. We had the rim of a barrel tacked onto the porch for a basketball hoop. And we played baseball with a hard rubber ball. We didn't have a bat, but we would get a tomato stake, and that would be a fine and dandy bat. We just had a big time.

Another game we played, we would dig holes in the yard and play tin-can fight. We'd get a can and crush it up, and everybody would stand by their hole with a stick. And one person was out and if he could get that can in your little hole. Then you would have to be the one who would have to try to get the can into a hole. So it was a fight to try to keep the can out of your hole. If you hit him on the shin with the stick, that was all right too. You did whatever you had to do to keep that can out of your hole.

When we got a little bit older, on Saturday nights we'd build a big old bonfire. And my mother would make some cookies, and we'd have some Kool-Aid. And everybody would come, and we'd have a party around the fire. And we'd play kiss the judge and spin the bottle and things like that. We had ways to amuse ourselves.

We'd work all week long and stay at home picking, but on Saturday we got to go to town. That was the treat for the whole year. We'd usually, about noon, when we got our bale finished and in the pickup truck, go to town. The pickup had sideboards on it, and you'd put your cotton in and stomp it down and stomp it down some more and pack it. And then when it was full, that would make a bale. There were so many kids that my mother and my older sisters and my baby brother would ride in the cab, and myself and my older brother and my younger sister would ride on top of the bale out to Dumas. When we got there, Dumas probably had a population around six thousand, but there would be at least twice that many on the streets on Saturday. There were so many people you couldn't walk down the street. There were a lot of Mexicans there with big old huge hats, and I remember being fascinated by these people that talked funny and had these big hats. But my mother wouldn't let me stand and gawk. She would push me along, push me along, and my daddy would take me to the movie. That was a big deal.

There was a movie theater on Main Street, and there was always a western movie. I would get a quarter, and we would sometimes go over to Bud's and get a hamburger for a nickel and then to the movie and get a coke for a nickel and a candy bar. After the movie we would go to the grocery store on Main Street and get groceries, and we would get tuna fish, and that was such a treat because that would be the only time of the year we would get tuna fish, when we picked cotton and had some money. Mother would get fifty pounds of flour and fifty pounds of meal and sugar, stuff that she couldn't grow. And one thing that we had that was such a treat at the time, she would get spaghetti, something we didn't usually have. We got Sunbeam light bread and that was a treat, to get bought bread, something besides homemade biscuits and cornbread. That light bread, the baloney, the tuna fish especially were a treat.

The streets would be extremely crowded. People were visiting. There had been a big migration of people from the hill country of the state who had moved down during the depression so that was the opportunity for them to all get together and see people they had grown up with and had affection for. All of my mother's family, as well as my dad's family, had moved to Desha County from the hills. Without fail they went to Dumas on Saturdays, and they would stay until bedtime.

Also, everybody got together on the weekends and went to each others' house to visit. That's what you did for entertainment. You didn't sit around and watch a football game or anything else. The kids would go outside and play. They'd play ball or whatever, and if they were older, they would talk and try to get together.

Bill Covey

We were poor, but it was a good life. We were all free. We didn't have stress. You didn't worry about whether your clothes were as good as those of the kid in the desk next to you because most of us wore overalls anyway. We did pretty much as we pleased. There were parameters that we stayed within, and you could do pretty much what you wanted to as long as you stayed within them. If you stepped outside them, your rear was warmed up.

I don't' recall anyone ever telling me snakes would bite you. I remember seeing rattle snakes, whole dens of them. You were expected to know, and I guess we did. We'd go frog-gigging over on Joneses Lake regularly. Some of the biggest bullfrogs I've ever seen were in there. We fished the Blue Hole, and it was our favorite swimming hole.

I went squirrel hunting at six, seven, eight, nine. The adults would take us into the woods and leave us in a spot where we were supposed to stay while they went further in. Used a .22 and later a .412 shotgun. I was allowed a single shot until I was about fourteen and could have an automatic. We would whistle quails up and shoot them with a .22.

School was closed for deer season, and we hunted deer. You learned to be decisive; you had to be. You had to make decisions. Since there was nobody out there taking care of you, you had to be responsible for yourself.

At recess we played tag and shot marbles if you could keep the big guys from coming along and stealing your marbles with their toes. Another game we had was when one boy would get on another's back and then we would try to pull each other off, and the last pair standing was the winner.

We didn't have a gym, but we played baseball and basketball. We played basketball competitively with other schools even though we played outside. I remember my very first ball glove. I wrote a jingle for Pepsi-Cola and got ten dollars for it and bought a ball glove. I must have been about twelve.

When I was a teenager, we hitchhiked all over the place and weren't scared at all. I wouldn't do it now and wouldn't let my kids do it either. Things changed when dope started, I think.

For dancing you would go to a bridge and line all the trucks up and put the headlights on the bridge and turn all the radios to the same radio station for music. There'd be anywhere from five trucks to twelve or fourteen trucks just loaded with people, sometimes thirty, forty, fifty kids.

They used to have the Rabbit's Foot Minstrel in a tent on the east edge of Dumas. They had blackface minstrels and chorus girls and comedians and everything else. It always happened in the fall when there was more money, and everybody went from the drudgery of picking cotton to the lightness in life. Everybody went; you could hardly get in.

There were also tent movies. I remember seeing *Two Years before the Mast* with Alan Ladd. One year for sure, roller skating came in the same way, in a tent. They had prefabricated floor sections bolted together. They rented the skates: a quarter to get in and a quarter for renting skates.

I want the world to know that I can't think of a better place to have been reared.

We made our own fun.

At recess we jumped rope and learned all the rhymes you learned in those days and the girls played house between the roots of a huge old oak tree. I remember making things out of the tops of acorns and scraping the dirt and setting up little rooms. We played hop scotch depending on the season and we played chase. There were some swings and a couple of seesaws and probably some monkey bars, but I don't remember playing on them.

In the neighborhood we roller skated a lot and rode our bicycles. I would get on my bicycle, and I could ride all over town if I wanted to, and I never remember being fussed at or even asked where I had gone. Probably somebody did, but it was never an issue.

We played outdoors every minute we could. Mother would make us come in in the summertime and rest between one and three. And Marianna didn't have a swimming pool, so to go swimming we had to go to Forrest City, and that was a big treat. Sometimes Daddy would take us out to swim at the L'anguille, at the cutoff. Dirty water, I can't believe we did that but we did. It was a swampy river, and I'm sure there was some talk about watching out for snakes in the river. We did go to Bear Creek as we got older, and it was much cleaner. In junior high and high school a bunch of kids would drive out to Bear Creek and go swimming. And we felt totally safe.

And we played out at night in the summertime until time to go to bed. It would be after dark. We made up games and would play kick the can and piggy in the pen wants a motion, and then we made up a game called Germans where you captured and tied the enemy up. We had a lot of kids in the neighborhood, and because there were so many kids, people from other neighborhoods would come and play with us. So we had ball games going, touch football, I remember lemonade in the street at night. I remember making streetcars out of shoeboxes and putting candles in them and dragging them down the street at night.

We loved it when the city would send somebody to flush out the fire hydrants. and we would all put on bathing suits and go out and get wet. We took shower baths in the rain, dammed up the gutters, followed the ice wagon.

When it snowed, it was wonderful because near our house there was McCullough's Hill and McCullough's Pond. And in the summertime we loved to catch turtles there, but in the wintertime we sledded on that hill. On the back side it had a little jump, and you could go over it and land. And nobody ever worried about us getting hurt. Kids did these things. If the pond froze over, we could slide down the other side of the hill and slide across the pond. It very rarely happened that it would freeze solidly enough for us to do that. I remember playing shinny on that pond, like ice hockey without skates. It was just playing, just being outside and playing. I feel like kids miss so much these days because they just don't have the freedom or the safety. We didn't have television or air conditioning. We just played outside and had a great time. When it was too hot to be outside and between one and three in the afternoon, we played Monopoly on the side porches.

In the wintertime my neighbors, a girl a year older on one side and a girl three years older on the other side and I would play paper dolls. I had an aunt who was an artist, and she would draw the dolls, and we would design and make the clothes for them. We made up games from radio serials and cartoons. We just made up stuff a lot.

And one of my best memories of when I was about ten my Mother let my sister and me walk down to the Marianna Hotel and buy our own supper. We had bacon, lettuce, and tomato sandwiches, and I think chocolate milk. And then walked down two doors to the movie by ourselves, and we felt so grown up to get to do that. We saw Doris Day and Jack Carson in *Romance on the High Seas*. Then we called Mother, and she came and picked us up.

We started dating very early. By the time I was in the eighth grade, I was dating a boy in the tenth, and he got his family car and probably was just fifteen. I was probably thirteen when I had my first kiss and steady boyfriend, which was way too young. I look back and really regret a lot of that because I grew up feeling that my identity was tied up with having a boyfriend. The popular girls had boyfriends. We did a lot of riding around because there wasn't much else to do. We had a lot of dancing. There were dances after the home games, and then from the time I was in the seventh grade all the way through high school at Christmas and at special occasions, somebody's parents would rent the community-house ballroom, and we would have a formal dance where you wore an evening dress and got corsages and the boys got boutonnieres. We danced to the juke box. The only time we ever had a band was the junior-senior prom, but I went to my first junior-senior prom when I was in the ninth grade. The prom was in the gym at the high school. The junior class decorated it, and the junior class mothers put on the banquet for the seniors in the cafeteria. But I remember driving when I was thirteen. You know, everybody was just driving cars.

Levon Helm

For a kid like me, looking to have fun and raise a little hell on a cotton farm, resources were somewhat limited. You had to work with what you had. For my purposes, this proved to be my daddy's Allis-Chalmers tractor. I'd take that old three-wheeler with the disk cutter on the back of it, put it in high gear, and had a hell of a lot of fun running tractor wheelies across a cotton field. That disk brought the tractor's front end up in the air, so if you popped your clutch *just right* you could run for acres out there on two wheels.

High gear, wide open. You'd see that drainage ditch coming, so you picked up that disk nice and smooth. The side of the drainage ditch was the closest thing we had to a hill, and you'd hit it with that front end and force it in the air, bounce it up, run twenty yards on the back wheels. It couldn't turn over because the disk was there.

I'd stand up during these stunts, just to make my dad crazy. I'd be coming around the corner, about to hit the turn row on two wheels, and I'd see J. D. jumping and waving by the gas tank, trying to get me to stop. Wide open: Hit the clutch, hit one of the brakes, and start skipping up to that gas tank where old J. D. is having a fit, and at the last moment, flop that disk. Fooomp! All stop. (29)

Terry Shoffner

There were ten to twelve kids I played with. The instructions from my parents were always: watch out for the snakes and be careful crossing the highway. That was all; there was less to worry about then. One of the play places for us where we spent a lot of time was a drainage ditch where we patched up an old boat, and of course there were water moccasins and such there. We played a lot of sports through high school, more of a pickup game situation with a variety of ages of kids. We would get together on a vacant lot and play baseball and football, totally unstructured.

I loved growing up in the country. I had some freedoms that I see my son doesn't have in the city. You'd just go out for the day. We didn't have electronic distractions, didn't even have television until I was eight or nine and then got maybe three channels. So we entertained ourselves different ways. I built model airplanes. We had a little workshop with a vise and a handsaw and a hammer, and we built a lot of our toys. A lot of the reason I became an artist was from watching and mimicking my brother who was good with his hands, a real craftsman.

One of the toys poor kids had was rolling an old tire. Some people could even do a tire with each hand. There was a large barn behind our house. Huge. It was turned into an auction house, so there were extensive pens behind the barn for weekly cattle auctions. When sales were not on, we would walk the top of the fence. It was almost like wire walking. We got good enough to play tag on it. The fence went all over the place. The upstairs in the barn was for hay storage. We would build tunnels in the hay by stacking the bales. That was a big place to play. On sale days I would go to the barn and hang out then come home for lunch and go back again.

My dad bought me a horse when I was ten or twelve, a slow,

gentle fourteen-year-old horse. The horse and I would go out, and my dog would go with us for my protection. We grew up together.

Cecile Cazort Zorach

b. 1946, Little Rock, Pulaski County. University professor. Memory written for this collection, 2009.

I remember that we dressed up to go downtown on Saturday afternoons. I have an image of my mother with white gloves on in the bus—or did this come out of Flannery O'Connor? No, I'm sure she wore white gloves. This is plausible because I also clearly remember as a very small child that we would all put on dresses in the afternoon to sit on the porch. I don't think we would have ever gone down town in slacks.

The bus we took downtown was a trolley bus, with rods going along electric cables at the top. Going downtown was probably some blend of a public promenade and a slightly daring adventure rather than a matter of running errands. I don't remember ever buying much of anything. Once in a while we would buy something and Mama would have it sent out so that we didn't have to carry packages. Sometimes we'd go to the public library, a wonderful little Carnegie building with a stained glass domed skylight in the main reading room and a room in the basement with a large stuffed giraffe. The children's room was in the basement and we loved it. Why did they tear that building down? Was it really made of white marble?

There was an arcade downtown with shops that were enticing but not very practical. I'm sure there was an antiques place there, maybe even an art supply place. I don't know that we ever actually entered the shops, but just walking into that space, away from the street into a pedestrian zone inhabited by unconventional people—or so it seemed to me—seemed like a thrilling adventure. I was heartbroken when they tore it down, and to this day I rejoice in finding arcades in older US cities—Ann Arbor, several in Cleveland.

Another destination was the dentist. We had tried a young fellow out in our suburban neighborhood, but when he told my parents that I needed braces, they decided to stick with a more traditional old guy who had an office in one of the older downtown buildings. He was a lovely old man, Dr. Jim. I don't know whether he even knew about Novocain. We never had it. We just held up our hand when the drill started feeling "hot." He also didn't believe in regular toothpaste, recommending instead a salty tooth powder that was just horrible. But he had the nicest blue eyes and the sweetest manner so that I don't remember particularly minding going to him. And there was something exciting about going up four or five flights of stairs to see him. As we got older, we started to set up our own appointments and I remember the tears filling my eyes when I called up one day and learned that he had retired. To this day, I have very good, but very crooked teeth.

Jeannie Whayne

My dad raised greyhounds, so we always lived in the country, outside of town, wherever we lived. There just wasn't a lot to do out in the countryside. I actually associate living out in the country with my chosen profession as a historian because we weren't close to a library, so I would read whatever was at hand, sometimes dime novels that my father had, also text books. I started reading history textbooks. It was just from sheer boredom that I turned to whatever I had to read.

I remember those days in Lepanto and outside Marked Tree in the country as being very long and very boring. It was dull. Long days sitting on the porch or reading, reading—reading good, bad, and indifferent, whatever I could get my hands on. And we lived down a long gravel road so we would walk. There was a girl who lived across the road and another about a half mile down the road who were best buds, so my sister, Roberta, and I would go for long walks with them and talk and sing songs.

My mother would take us to swimming pools. She loved to swim, and we lived on the side of Marked Tree that made it more convenient to go to Truman than to Lepanto. So we would go to Truman, and usually one of my brother's friends would go with us, and we would go and have the time of our lives in that swimming pool. At some point in the early sixties it got closed because of integration. It was a great loss to us. It left a big hole in our lives because they couldn't conceive of having swimming pools with African American and white children swimming together. I thought it was stupid at the time, and it looks even stupider now.

While we were living outside of Marked Tree, I was in the 4-H Club for a little while, and the memory that sticks out the most about 4-H Club was learning how to shoot a .22 rifle. I already knew how to shoot because my father had taught us all how to shoot a handgun. And my brother tells this story, I'm not sure it's true, that I was a dead-eye with the .22, and my father, the gambler, used to bet on me, used to take me out in the woods with some men, and they wouldn't believe this little twelve year-old- girl could shoot.

Kathy Mandrell Vanlaningham

b. 1951, Paragould, Greene County. University administrator. Interview with Margaret Bolsterli, 2010.

We really didn't listen to music at home. I was a TV baby. TV had come along by the time I was growing up, and we had a TV in the kitchen while we ate dinner. We had a TV in the living room, and I grew up on Sky King and Roy Rogers and My Friend Flicka. So in our home, really, we didn't listen to music. Even for my grandparents, music was not a big thing in their lives. They would go around sometimes to what they called singings of gospel music.

Music didn't happen for me until I got into high school and started, like everybody else, listening to rock and roll, in the daytime, at WNPS out of Memphis. All the good stuff. And then at night, their power would go down, and we would pick up WLS out of Chicago. So I spent years hearing about the temperature in the Loop, and I had no idea what the Loop was. We were fortunate in that we had a band living in Paragould. At the time I knew them, and I interviewed them for my high school newspaper. They were called Nobody Else. When they got bigger, they changed their name to Black Oak Arkansas. They played frequently around Paragould. We would have dances at the VFW hall, but for the most part the bands were other high school guys trying to sound like them.

We had dances every weekend. It was the thing to do. And we had bands come from Jonesboro, and occasionally we would have a big to-do, somebody like the Boxtops from Memphis. I remember they put out a song called "The Letter" that you could hear on the radio, and to have somebody come you could hear on the radio was a very big deal. But we also, starting in high school, would go to shows in Memphis at the Mid-South Coliseum. I saw James Brown and several big names there. Sometimes a carload of us would get together and go.

When I graduated from high school, that summer of '69, that summer of Woodstock, a number of the groups that had done Woodstock went to other pop festivals, and one was just outside Baton Rouge called The New Orleans Pop Festival. And my brother, Bill, talked Mother into letting me go. So he and I and two of his friends went down there where I saw Janis Joplin, Jefferson Airplane, Country Joe and the Fish.

Karen Rudolph Shoffner

As kids we played in the neighborhood. I think it was typical of the times, the fifties. We played on the streets. We played on the school ground. It was rocky, and we used the rocks to build forts. Everything seemed to be forts, as I look back. There were sides: a winning and a losing to it. We threw rocks a lot. But the softer games we played if friends were over after school would be hopscotch, a lot of mother may I? Hide and seek and kick the can were summertime night games.

We played until somebody's parents screamed; dark wasn't usually the cut-off.

We were never allowed to cross the highway a block away, but we could roam around town, and we were free to walk to the city park. There were woods down at the end of our street. We could go down in there, but there were copperheads, and you had to be careful. This isn't an area where you can go out in the woods without being cautious. Lots of snakes. You just learned to be careful. It was a city existence. Girl Souts was a big deal because it was an organization with actual activities. We spent a lot of time working on badges. I'm sure we cheated all over the place to see who could get the most. You got to line up and march.

There were a lot of cultural events around the university. It wasn't at all uncommon to go up to the university museum to hang out for a while. The museum was on the fourth floor of Old Main, and you got off the elevator right at the entrance to the bell tower, and they would let you stand there and watch while they rang tunes on the bells. It was deafening but exciting.

Mothers were mostly home at that time and if you misbehaved, you were caught. But most of the time we were left alone. As I recall, in nice weather, we were outside during the day, came home for lunch and then were outside until dinnertime. Our job was to play. We didn't have household chores like washing the dishes, until we were a little older.

We played in the house a lot during colder weather. We played a lot of board games, card games, and we played with dolls a lot. I remember getting a Barbie doll in the third grade. It was a new doll and a big deal. It was a matter of changing clothes. You took the clothes off and put them on and took them off again and put them on.

We took lessons of every kind, piano lessons, and had to practice every day. From the age of about seven or eight, we went to cotillion at the Episcopal church. Somebody came in and had a cotillion for kids where we got dressed up in party dresses, and the boys dressed up in their suits, and we had our manners polished. They would teach us things like knowing to stand when an adult came in the room. You filed by the refreshment table, and the little boys carried your refreshments and pulled out your chair for you. And they taught us ballroom dancing. They taught us things like the bunny hop, the fox trot, to waltz. Wednesday afternoons, I took art lessons.

There were community concerts at the university that my parents took us to. There were plays and operas held in the men's gym. Everybody would get dressed up in our Sunday clothes and sit in the bleachers and watch these marvelous productions.

In junior high we danced to early Chad and Jeremy. Very gentle music, coming up to the Beatles stuff. What you spent your money on was 45s. You could go to Guisinger's music store on the square and listen to 45s before you bought them. I have a sense it was a several-hour event but probably not. I can't imagine them tolerating anyone staying there that long.

Martha Conner McNair

We lived on a cotton farm about eight or nine miles from Augusta. We were one mile from Fitzhugh, where there was a gin and a store where we got our mail. The daughter of a black woman named Rosetta, who worked for my Dad, was in charge of looking after me, and her name was Irma Wren. And her brother, whose name was Gene Autry Wren, looked after my brother, and so whatever we did, they had to follow us around. I don't remember how much older Irma was than I was at the time, but in her teens at the most. So Irma and Gene Autry and my brother and I would ride a horse that a friend of my father's brought for us, and we had kind of a little pasture in the back of our house that we played in and a barn that used to hold livestock and a storage barn and a shop. So there were always outbuildings we could be in and out of all the time and little shacks not far from us where black people lived that we would be in and out of. And we played in the trailers that had cotton in them, but you had to be very careful and you had to tell someone when you were getting in them because there were all sorts of horror stories of people getting covered up in the cotton and suffocating. There were dire warnings. You could tell the difference in people's voices when they were talking about it. I remember that Irma had total authority except when we took it, and then Irma would have to do what we wanted to do. But for the most part, we didn't do that. If Irma said, "We are going in," we went in.

I saw Irma not long ago. She was working in the hospital where my mother was, and we fell on each other, and just kept staring at each other, remembering from forty years ago.

Ruth, the woman who brought me up, entertained us a lot in ways that are gone. She would have us sit on the ground and plait grass. I guess we would do that while she did something else. It's bound to have been the way she taught her own children to plait their hair.

There was a family of white children not far away with three children also, and we were very good friends. But we didn't walk to their house. It was either too far or we were too young, I don't exactly know. But we played. We played in the woods. We fixed up a tree with a big old limb that bounced, and so that was a cool place to play during the summer. My brother would catch bumble bees and put them on strings. We just did anything we wanted to.

In Newport, we had lessons after school, piano and dance—ballet and tap and then, in the summer of course, Bible School that was in this enormous house that my aunt had left to the Methodist church because nobody wanted it. Daddy said who in the world would want it. It had eleven fireplaces! And then later the mother of one of my friends, who also taught the tap and ballet had a little cotillion when we were in junior high, but it wasn't much of one, just basics. It must not have been too frequent because I can't remember it very well.

The school had dances and the Methodist church had dances but the Baptists and the Church of Christ did not. And the Legion Hut had dances. Little did we know that the Silver Moon was there and Jerry Lee Lewis and Elvis Presley and other up-and-comers were out there playing, but I didn't go into the Silver Moon 'til I was thirty. You just couldn't; it was just a roadhouse. They have renamed that highway now "Rock and Roll Highway" because of all these people that just started out in all those little roadhouses along there. My people thought Elvis Presley was absolute trash. I can still remember sitting in front of my grandmother's house, we would go to my grandmother's house every Sunday night and have Welsh rabbit and some sort of dessert that the cook, Mattie, had left. And I remember sitting out in front before we got out of the car, and "Blue Suede Shoes" came on the radio, and my dad said, "Who in the world would listen to that who could listen to B. B. King." I was thirteen when the Beetles came to America, and that's where my friends and I began. I don't remember thinking about Elvis Presley one way or the other. I didn't like him. Still don't.

Julie Gabel

There were no other children on our street, so I would do a lot of playing by myself. I recall playing outside a lot. The neighbors were older couples, and they would let me do pretty much whatever I wanted to do. I had imaginary friends. I would play gardening. I would play with a ball, a stick. There weren't that many outdoor toys like there are now. You would just kind of make it up as you went along. I made mud pies and little rock forts and stuff like that. I loved to climb trees, and since my mother liked to dress me in dresses, she would make panties, often ruffled panties, to match my dresses. There was one tree in particular in our front yard that I loved to climb. . . . I would usually take dolls up there and leave them, and after a hearty wind you might see several dolls lying at the bottom of the tree. They looked like casualties.

And directly behind my mother and dad's house on Hall Avenue, just a block over was Sunset. And between the back of the properties on both streets, there was a strip of land that was a farm that belonged to the Halls, and when I was five or six I remember going over there a lot to play. There was just this rickety old fence that I could hop over to get there. And directly behind our house was their barn, and they had one horse and one or two milk cows, at different times. They had a few chickens in the chicken house. And they had a little cream-ery where they could separate the milk from the cream. I think they sold the milk. I remember that Mr. Hall would let me come over and help because I knew not to get directly behind the horse, and he could trust me around the animals. I would ride the horse some and play with the cow, and they had tons of cats, maybe thirty cats, indoor and outdoor. . . . Those cats were everywhere. Mrs. Hall was kind of a large woman and so sweet, so nice. I played over there quite a bit because I like animals.

We went out to my granddad's farm a lot and rode horses, so I had both worlds. I could just take the horse and go out by myself. We had a cutting horse, and he would just start making little pods of cows. I could just go out there and spend hours doing nothing: picking the locust shells off the side of the smokehouse and feeding the horses and combing them and bathing them, going up in the loft of the barn. I saw kittens born up in the loft of my granddad's barn. I think I got a lot of that slow-paced being inquisitive about nature and things at the farm, and then we lived in town so there was that, as well. So I think I particularly got a nice, well-grounded life. And my mom was especially sensitive about the things I liked. They were huge sports fans, but that was never pushed on me. My mother had a nice voice and sang some, and she kept asking me if I wanted to try different things, like dance. I took tap and then ballet.

Lillie Mae Fears

We played games at my grandmother's. Indoors we had talent shows. I guess we got it from Ed Sullivan. She had this big open door with a curtain you could slide across and we would have serious talent shows where you would come out and perform and we'd all be sitting there then we'd close the curtain until the next act. We had a piano in the house, and my aunt Judith taught herself to play little songs. And she would teach me to play these little songs, and as a little kid she would have the words to them and sing.

We were outside a lot. It never got too hot. We just played forever. We would play kickball, and we had a little bridge across the ditch in front of my grandparents' house where we would have graduation ceremonies. We loved to make mudpies, some pretty sophisticated stuff. We'd play store and sell things, just make believe out of the world. We played mother may I. And we played, "Mariddle, Mariddle, Marie, I see something you don't see, and it is . . . And now you have to guess what I'm talking about," and when you finally get it right, you get to say it. We had plenty of games.

When I was in elementary school, I always sat there looking forward to coming home and playing with my brothers and sisters. I always played teacher. I was never into dolls and things. I had to be teacher. I joke with my brothers and sister that I kept them in second grade when they were in fifth and sixth because I would force them to play with me. We were real close knit.

When we were teenagers and my cousins would come down from Chicago and Seattle and New Orleans for the summers, we would have our groupies with Michael Jackson and the Jackson Five, and we'd sit around and watch Soul Train and Good Times. Of course everybody always knew the latest dances. We watched Soul Train religiously—it's kind of like another version of American Bandstand where most of the guests are black—and tried to copy some of those dances.

Then we got a skating rink, and skating became the big thing because that was a lot safer than going to some night club, some hole in the wall with smoke and people who don't mean you any good. The skating rink was a really big hit. We had two skating rinks in Helena and West Helena. When I was in the eleventh and twelfth grades, we started having dances at the school. You had to be thirteen to get in. We'd get the local DJ and charge a dollar admission.

Michael Thomas

I had three really good friends in Farmington, and we played outside a lot. Playing in that neighborhood was nice. I still like driving through there every once in a while, for the memories. It had a creek that kids played in, and it had a wooded area. There were houses being built that were great fun to play in. We would play in those houses they were building after the workers left.

And I had a little transistor radio that I loved. I would strap it to the handle bars of my bike. Michael Jackson was big, and I would turn it up real loud and ride around the neighborhood 'til my friends heard it and would come out. And then we'd go off to the woods together. We found a bunch of stray dogs one time living out by the creek down there, a mom and a batch of puppies. We took them food and took care of them for a while, and the mom would let us near them. One guy's mom didn't want us around them, told us not to be going around them because they might have rabies. To us, though, it was this great thing; we had our own pets, all of a sudden. But she went down and shot them with a .22 rifle. And that memory stands out very strongly.

We became little businessmen in that neighborhood. I remember we went beyond the lemonade stand. We had a lot of scrap wood because of the construction sites. We took wood out of their burn pile and built a tree house down by the creek, and then we built a little stand where we sold Kool-Aid. We thought Kool-Aid would be more popular than lemonade, so we did pretty well. And then we opened a popcorn stand. I realized that to run a business you've got to have a gimmick. You can't just sell lemonade or water so we had colored popcorn, and when it popped, of course, the top was white, but you could see the color in the kernel. So we put it in little bags and sold it for nickel or a dime. And then at dusk we had magic shows in this same little booth. And then we set up multiple stands. We had two or three stands in different places. Our customers were other kids, usually kids younger than us, and older brothers who thought what we were doing was cool. I would ride my bike around and check on things and make more Kool-Aid and popcorn. But it got to be too much and wasn't any fun anymore.

I remember the bully in the neighborhood, a stereotypical bully named Rex. We were playing at the creek one time, and he said he was supposed to count to ten before he hit anybody. And one time he said to me, "You got water on my watch, c'mere." So he counted to ten and hit me hard enough to loosen a tooth. Hit me right in the mouth. It happened so quick and hurt so bad I was kind of in shock and I walked off and went home, but first I went to his house and told his mom, and she chased him down and whipped him. And I went on home with a loose tooth that was bleeding. I didn't like to fight. I think that's when I developed a sense of humor and learned to joke my way out of bad situations.

CONCLUSION

So what conclusions are to be drawn from the varied accounts related here of growing up in Arkansas on the cusp of electronic diversions? The world changed between 1890 and 1980, and the purpose here has been to make observations, not value judgments, about the changes. To say "this is what it was like, this is what we did," not "the way we spent our time was better or worse before modern conveniences like washing machines, radios, television, computers and cell phones were invented." For in spite of the genuine regret at the loss of communication and closeness within families and communities of people who shared so much, including adversity, one of the undeniable aspects of these accounts is that people were excited about new conveniences that brought them entertainment and relief from backbreaking labor and boredom. They wanted their world to change and welcomed the changes. While those who worked in the fields all find some affirmation in the hardship they endured, they all also say they would not want their children to have to do it.

Testimony to the nostalgia that people feel for those long-gone days of what now look like deprivation and drudgery is the prevalence of annual reunions on the school grounds of schools long lost to consolidation in communities that now barely exist, like Kingston in Madison County and the Watson Fish Fry in Desha County, that draws a thousand people every summer.

Another inescapable conclusion to be drawn is that while adversity undeniably does kill the spirit and ruin the lives of countless children, sometimes it provides the spark that ignites a burning ambition. Proof of this is the large number of successful people in all fields who share some of the memories collected here of deprivation and, at times, a seeming desert of educational opportunity. "We made our own entertainment," they say over and over, and they might well have said also, "We made our own opportunities."

As for the effect growing up in Arkansas had on Arkansans, many of those quoted here mentioned in their interviews that they would not have wanted to grow up anywhere else. I think the reason was eloquently expressed by the journalist Roy Reed, who grew up in Garland County, left in 1948 for college in Missouri, and then worked for *The Arkansas Gazette* and *The New York Times* and traveled all over the world. He and his wife, Norma, moved from London, England, to Hogeye in Washington County in 1979. This is what he said when I asked him in an interview in 1997 why he came back:

> I've lived outside of Arkansas I suppose more than I've lived in it. But always, wherever I was, Detroit or Washington or wherever I happened to be, whenever we headed home to Arkansas by car, Norma and I used to kid about it: "Well, we're getting close to the Memphis-Arkansas Bridge," or wherever we were about to cross the line into Arkansas. And we built this illusion that once we set foot on Arkansas soil nothing could happen to us. That is, if we had car trouble, somebody would take care of us. If it was in the middle of the night, somebody would take us in. Because we were back home, if you can call that a definition of home, built as it was on pure air. If we'd landed in West Memphis near the dog track, they would probably have run us in, but there's always that feeling that if I could just get back to Arkansas, I would be at home, home being, of course, where I was born and brought up. And as far as I can tell, this is totally irrational. I'm sure I could be happy in any of twenty-five places around the world, but this is the one that feels like home.

INFORMANTS

NAME	OCCUPATION	HOME COUNTY	PAGES
Abbott, Shirley	writer, editor	Garland	29, 52, 123
Angelou, Maya	writer, actor, dancer, professor	Lafayette	7, 13
Bell, Beatrice Sharp	housewife	Madison	72
Bennett, Gerald	farmer	Madison	9, 35, 99, 121
Boone, Holly	writer	Sebastian	60
Bowen, William H.	retired lawyer, banker, dean	Jefferson	12, 74, 99, 121
Cash, Johnny,	musician	Mississippi	xviii, 41
Covey, Bill	retired army officer	Desha	xviii, 80, 126
Elders, Joycelyn	physician, former surgeon general	Howard	xviii, 15, 45, 78, 101
Fears, Lillie Mae	professor	Phillips	87, 111, 140
Feaster, LaVerne	retired head of state 4-H Clubs	Woodruff	xviii, 10, 56, 97, 119
Ferguson, Randall, Jr.	retired business executive	Ouachita	23, 57, 107
Gabel, Julie	IT administrator	Washington	62, 110, 139

NAME	OCCUPATION	HOME COUNTY	PAGES
Gladden, Zeraldine Daniel	Businesswoman	Yell, Desha	73
Helm, Levon	musician, actor	Phillips	48, 79, 102, 130
Hogan, Phydella	retired music store owner	Washington	36, 96
Hudson, Fritz	retired farmer	Lincoln	8, 100, 122
Hudson, Joy Nuckols	retired high school teacher	Desha	xviii, 40, 122
Johnson, Sally Stockley	retired teacher, minister	Lee	xviii, 16, 24, 128
Jones, Robert E.	retired businessman	Desha	38, 121
Katz, Pearl Lou Mattmiller	housewife	Arkansas	14, 32, 68, 94, 118
Kearney, Janis Faye	writer, editor, publisher, personal diarist to President Bill Clinton	Lincoln	85, 108
Maulden, Jerry	retired business executive	Pulaski	xviii, 26, 47
McNair, Martha Conner	high school teacher	Woodruff/ Jackson	20, 105, 137
Pace, Bonnie	retired high school teacher	Madison	70
Parker, Leta Drake	housewife, farmer	Madison	5, 34, 95
Pennington, Helen	retired insurance agent	Desha	xviii, 82, 103, 124

NAME	OCCUPATION	HOME COUNTY	PAGES
Peter, Lily	planter, poet, ginner, philanthropist	Phillips	92
Reed, Roy	journalist, professor	Garland	146
Riggins, Raymond	retired sales executive	Desha/ Lincoln	xviii, 25, 44, 75, 100, 121
Riley, Billy Lee	musician	Mississippi	xviii, 9, 24, 39, 77
Robertson, Mary Elsie	writer, professor	Franklin	58
Shoffner, Karen Rudolph	financial consultant	Washington	xviii, 23, 58, 84, 135
Shoffner, Terry	artist, professor	Jackson	xviii, 23, 58, 84, 135
Still, William Grant,	composer, musician	Pulaski	11, 33, 93
Stockley, Grif	attorney, writer	Lee	17, 53, 81
Thomas, Michael	teacher, writer, actor	Washington	62, 89, 113, 142
Vanlaningham, Kathy Mandrell	university administrator	Greene	134
Whayne, Jeannie	professor	Poinsett/ White	22, 27, 51, 83, 133
Willis, Delta	writer, communications director for the Audubon Society of America	Desha	xviii, 54
Zorach, Cecile Cazort	professor	Pulaski	xviii

MARGARET JONES BOLSTERLI is the author of *Born in the Delta* and *During Wind and Rain* and the editor of *Vinegar Pie and Chicken Bread* and *A Remembrance of Eden.* She is professor emerita of English at the University of Arkansas.